Compliance Cop to Culture Coach

Compliance Cop to Culture Coach

Examining the Why, How, and What

William A. Sommers and Jakub Grządzielski

ROWMAN & LITTLEFIELD
Lanham • Boulder • New York • London

Published by Rowman & Littlefield
An imprint of The Rowman & Littlefield Publishing Group, Inc.
4501 Forbes Boulevard, Suite 200, Lanham, Maryland 20706
www.rowman.com

86-90 Paul Street, London EC2A 4NE

Copyright © 2023 by William A. Sommers and Jakub Grządzielski

All rights reserved. No part of this book may be reproduced in any form or by any electronic or mechanical means, including information storage and retrieval systems, without written permission from the publisher, except by a reviewer who may quote passages in a review.

British Library Cataloguing in Publication Information Available

Library of Congress Cataloging-in-Publication Data

ISBN 9781475868616 (cloth)
ISBN 9781475868623 (paperback)
ISBN 9781475868630 (electronic)

We dedicate this book to Frank Wagner and Jathan Janove. Both have contributed to our learning and growth as coaches and have been critical partners in extending our learning to others. We are deeply grateful and honor their work in the field of leadership, coaching, and organizational development. We say a big mahalo!

Contents

Foreword	ix
Acknowledgments	xiii
Chapter 1: Introduction	1
SECTION I: THE "WHY"	9
Chapter 2: Some Basics of Leadership	11
SECTION II: THE "HOW"	17
Chapter 3: The Seven Cs of Learning Cultures	19
Chapter 4: Communication	29
Chapter 5: Facilitating Collaboration	33
Chapter 6: Coaching and Supervision	37
Chapter 7: Conflict and What You Can Do about It	49
Chapter 8: NAvigATiNg The rAPids of ChaNge	65
Chapter 9: Creativity	69
Chapter 10: Courage	77
SECTION III: THE "WHAT"	83
Chapter 11: Cultural Competence	85
Chapter 12: Coaching Tools	93

Chapter 13: Commonwealth   99
Conclusion: Next Steps   105

Index   107
About the Authors   111

Foreword

Culture has always been at the forefront in the field of anthropology. In the fields of business and leadership, it was always there but largely overlooked. This situation began to change with the publication of a groundbreaking book titled *In Search of Excellence* in 1982. Written by Tom Peters and Robert H. Waterman Jr., this book culminated the internal work of McKinsey & Company. In this study, they examined a sample of companies that were considered excellent based on a long history of profitability, industry leadership, and seemingly having plans to stay on top.

What they found consistent among these companies were eight themes, or characteristics. These themes were as follows: a bias for action; staying close to the customer; autonomy and entrepreneurship; productivity through people; hands-on, value driven, stick to their knitting; simple form; lean staff; and simultaneously loose-tight. Together, all of these are elements of a company's "culture." The popularity of this book spurned a heightened awareness of the importance of culture. It also led to the formation of a new industry of consultants specializing in helping organizations build and maintain a healthy culture.

This brings me to why I am writing this foreword to *Compliance Cop to Culture Coach*. I have known Bill Sommers for many years and Jakub Grządzielski for about four years. What the two of them have in common is that both attended our coach training and certification in Stakeholder Centered Coaching®. As the name implies, this is a methodology that recognizes the importance of stakeholders as coaches. When implemented widely, this process becomes part of the organization's culture.

What continues to impress me about Bill is his dedication to continuous learning, through both his experience in the trenches of the US educational systems and his insatiable appetite for the printed word. No one I know has read more leadership books than Bill, and he has written summaries of all of them. Years ago, he built a network of fellow learners he named the Learning Omnivores. The common use of the term relates to animals that eat everything. The word stems from the Latin word *omnis*, meaning "all or everything."

I won't claim this book covers everything when it comes to understanding and influencing organizational culture. What I will claim is the framework that makes up the core of this book offers a useful insight based on the seven Cs that support a learning culture. Taken together, these seven competencies—all starting with the letter "C"—help to equip leaders to influence culture from a certain mindset and set of skills—hence the title of this book. The most effective leaders have always approached their role as one to enable everybody to be part of the stewardship of their collective culture. The leader's role is to cultivate the culture instead of forcing it on others: in other words, become a culture coach instead of a compliance cop.

What has led these two authors to synthesize their knowledge and experience into this seven Cs model? They both come from different, yet similar, backgrounds based on being in unstable and turbulent times. Bill, through the formative years of profession, has been the principal of troubled high schools and middle schools. He has been brought into those schools that were in deep trouble and needed someone to turn the trajectory from outright failure to successfully serving the purpose inherent in these institutions. If you think your job as a leader is tough in your situation, it doesn't likely compare to a school that is floundering with disengaged teenagers being taught by hopeless teachers and distraught parents. Bill had done this job with remarkable results and then retired to consult. He has since been brought out of retirement a half-dozen times to rebuild another school and a revamped culture.

Jakub has a different, yet just as intriguing, base of experiences from his home in Poland. Jakub is an insightful and effective executive and leadership coach and organizational development consultant with a unique background as a former corporate executive and a master of engineering who meets other executives with a resonating voice of experience. In his career, Jakub successfully made the leap from a key production leader in a Top 10 Fortune Global 500 automotive company to his current position. Jakub's professional experience with the entire spectrum of management issues has provided him with a set of unique insights into successful management practices.

As both Bill and Jakub have honed their own leadership skills through their life experiences, you can benefit from what they know works throughout this book. Take any of the chapters devoted to one of the seven Cs, and you will find perspectives, thought exercises, and models that will equip you with learning you can apply to become a better culture coach. And you will find that much in these chapters is like "drinking through a fire hose." Do not try to absorb it all at one time. Some concepts, or frameworks, will resonate immediately. The light bulb for others might come after a few passes.

Finally, I'll say this book is worth it just for the volume of quotes from famous people. What I love about these quotes is they impart wisdom in a nanosecond and, when remembered, will guide you to contribute to the greater good for all.

Frank Wagner
Co-Founder of the Marshall Goldsmith Group
Stakeholder Centered Coaching
Author, leadership coach, former professor at UCLA

Acknowledgments

Bill and Jakub are grateful for the learning from three major sources.

Marshall Goldsmith continues to contribute to our knowledge, skills, and reflective practices. His writings, applications of concrete strategies, and ongoing support through videos and meetings have been invaluable to our own growth.

Frank Wagner, as the co-developer of Stakeholder Centered Coaching, remains gracious with ongoing support, practical ideas, and monthly phone calls to share with the SCC community his experience and skillful actions for us to use.

Chris Coffey, who has since passed, extended our growth as coaches through his real-life examples and clarity of the mission, and he will be deeply missed by the SCC coaches. Rest in peace, and thank you for sharing your gifts with us.

We also want to thank Tom Koerner, Carlie Wall, and the Rowman & Littlefield family for having the confidence to support this project and their direction, guidance, and support along the way.

Leslie Asher Blair has been a constant support by editing, suggesting, and doing final proofs. This book would not have been possible without her guidance.

Bill recognizes several people who have contributed to his growth as a coach and leadership developer. This is not an exhaustive list by any means:

- Jathan Janove, for his publications that are so well focused with effective strategies for use in real time.
- Betty Burks and Laura Robinson, who have been great collaborators as we move SCC into the educational field. We believe it could change school leadership for the better.
- Art Costa, who started me on a learning journey that I could never have imagined. Our ongoing conversations continue to inspire me. I love you.
- Marney Wamsley, the principal who kept me in education. I am grateful.

Jakub would like to direct his grateful thoughts to three fantastic people:

- Ron Meyer, for his mentorship and for instilling in me a passion for developing other people.
- Jaroslaw Stechowicz, for his life wisdom and generous willingness for sharing it with me.
- Szymon Piasecki, for his support and passion for true leadership.

Chapter 1

Introduction

Life is Change
Growth is Optional
Choose Wisely

—Karen Clark

Take a lesson from Marshall Goldsmith's book, *What Got You Here Won't Get You There* (2007). Most of us have learned from the people and processes that helped us reach this point in our personal and professional life. However, as the saying goes, "if you always do what you did, you will always get what you got."

Learning is Change, Change is Learning.

—Hord and Sommers (2007)

When world demographics, economies, and relationships change, remaining the same is probably not the best option. As life changes, we need to reassess the tactics and strategies we have been relying on to accomplish our goals. To paraphrase Darwin, survival goes to the most adaptable, not the fittest or toughest.

Adaptation to a changing environment is the way of the most productive individuals and organizations as well as the natural world. Very few companies that were industry leaders in the 1900s or even 2000s exist in the same form. Some do not exist because they resisted modifying their business strategy. Think of corporations like Polaroid, Kodak, Blockbuster, or VHS.

Companies and leaders announce and adhere to strong values to maintain focus and integrity. But as the world changes, how do individuals and organizations continuously adapt? This is such an important question that Lieutenant General Rick Lynch titled his book *Adapt or Die* (2013).

The acronym VUCA (volatility, uncertainty, complexity, ambiguity) keeps coming up in conversations about management. In a book titled *Get There Early*, Bob Johansen (2007) identified a graphic organizer to anticipate changes. The left side of figure 1.1 shows possible negative effects of VUCA. The right side provides some values for helping us lead through changing times:

- Vision
- Understanding
- Clarity
- Agility

One effective way to help leaders make positive changes that focus on the terms provided by the right side of the graphic is the Stakeholder Centered Coaching (SCC) developed by Marshall Goldsmith, Frank Wagner, and Chris Coffey. (Both authors of this book are certified Stakeholder Centered Coaches.) Leadership is critical in navigating changes in our lives and the cultures of the organizations where we work, especially in this current VUCA environment.

First, let's go over a few basics to prepare for our journey together. Many times, we focus on the negative performance of an individual or work group. As W. Edwards Deming posited years ago, look at the design of the organization that is getting results. What organizational systems may be contributing to the outcomes? What are the potentiators? What are the barriers? Have you talked to the individuals and work groups to obtain their point of view?

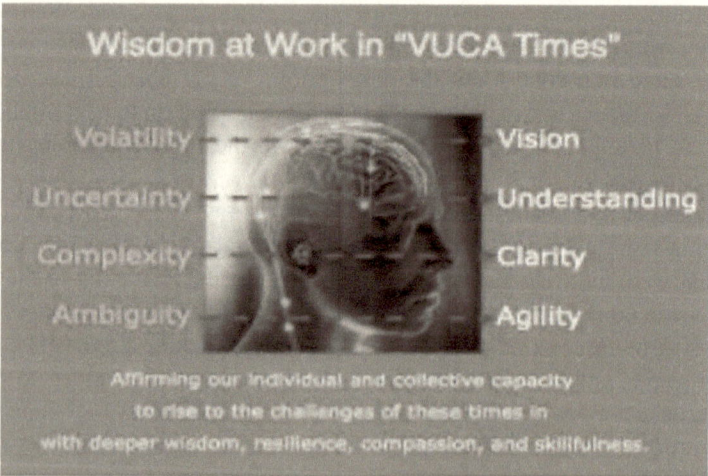

Figure 1.1

Richard Beckhard, adjunct professor at MIT, cited in Dannemiller and Jacobs (1992), developed the following model for change in systems:

$$D \times V \times FS > R$$

- There must be dissatisfaction (D) with the results or processes of the current state.
- A vision (V) of what is wanted in the future state.
- First steps (FS) on the plan or pathway to get to the vision.
- When those three elements are present and greater than the resistance (R) (or attraction to the status quo), change is possible.

There is one prerequisite, however. People must believe change is possible. When change doesn't seem possible or there has been a history of false starts, the past will need to be addressed first. Otherwise, the TTSP (this too shall pass) immune system takes over and will ultimately win.

Chris Coffey and David Lam, in *The New IQ* (2015), write that IQ should now stand for "Innovative Questions." So, throughout this book the reader will see new IQs. These IQs provide time to connect the information to your situation, to reflect about past events, and consider applying concepts to future decisions.

IQ: How would Beckhard's model have helped with changes in the past? How will you use Beckhard's model to plan change events in the future?

In *Managing Transitions*, William Bridges (1991) suggests there are three parts to the process:

- Endings—celebrate the end of a product, process, or change in personnel.
- Neutral zone—when people are asked to change, they lose something familiar. This throws people into an uncomfortable stage, uncertain that the familiar in the past is gone and uncertain of what the future holds. This stage is where leadership is crucial in calming fears, keeping the vision in full view, and supporting those making the changes.
- Beginnings—clearly define what is new and how the future is preferable to the past.

Vignette

When asked to take on turnaround assignments or to make changes in the system, honor the past, even though it might not have been a great experience.

It is important to celebrate those who worked hard to keep commitments for the goals of the company. In a school where I (Bill) was brought in to replace the leader, deal with layoffs resulting from failure to pass a levy referendum, and create positive morale, the first order of business was having the remaining staff communicate in an open meeting. The existing staff needed to know they were safe and had employment. One staff member was chosen to speak for each departed colleague.

After this public acknowledgment, the meeting took a break. I was introduced as the new leader. This provided the opportunity to set a vision for the future, provide background from the leader's experience, and give a chance for the existing staff to ask questions. That process helped the organization allay some of the concern and allowed us to move ahead faster. Change is not easy and not for the faint of heart. A leader must demonstrate competence and confidence.

IQ: How have change initiatives been done in the past? How might planning an ending, supporting people in the neutral zone, and creating a new beginning change the way new initiatives are received?

We would like to invite the reader to be open to possibilities and not be afraid to take the risk of putting leaders in the situations described in this book. Such an attitude will allow leaders to answer the question of how much they are ready for the changes taking place around them.

As you lead others in business or nonprofits, you can be sure of one thing: something is constantly changing. Interestingly, one looks in vain for the source of ongoing changes in profits. If you dig deep enough to meet the people around you, you will find that the necessity to express yourself is what drives the world and the ever-emerging changes. Therefore, by standing in the position of a leader who is afraid of the coming future and the changes related to it, you doom yourself and your team to failure. What we want to encourage you to do is start to see the necessity of self-expression as an amazing opportunity and an advantage. Great leaders embrace the change; in fact, they are actively pursuing it and looking ahead to the consequences of a changing world. This is undoubtedly due to their self-awareness, maturity in leading others, and the awareness that it is their responsibility to effectively lead a team or company through this process.

It doesn't matter what the change is for, it matters what the change does.

—Anonymous

Look at the change as a process, just like in any industry, and you will then be able to see individual milestones, transitions, and related changes. And just like in the case of a product's development, individual milestones, transitions, and related challenges. And just like in the case of a product's development, change takes on a completely different face at each of these stages, which in turn requires different behavior from the leader.

We assume that you may have already encountered a change for the sake of change, to make something twitch or to get out of stagnation. If you think this is a way of capturing change, you couldn't be more wrong.

Change, in its definition and essence, is something positive and promising, and there must be a greater cause behind it.

> Be the change that you wish to see in the world.
>
> —Mohandas Gandhi

Introducing a change is a conscious and responsible act, resulting from care for your subordinates and the belief that its implementation is necessary and right.

Imagine approaching your subordinate with these words: "I would like you to trust me and believe that, for our common good, we must make an extra effort over the next few months and go in the same direction under my guidance."

This is exactly what you are asking for when announcing a change. Are you always convinced that the reason for the change is worth mobilizing your team? Is this reason good enough to inspire them and make them see you as a reliable and competent leader over time?

Wishful thinking is no substitute for a great cause, compelling vision, and strategic plan.

Let an example of a profound reason for change be Steve Jobs's discussion with his executives as they left Xerox headquarters. That's when Jobs realized that although his new operating system was almost ready, it was necessary to cross out the entire project and start working on the graphical interface system. He realized that the conscious loss of millions of dollars invested in the operating system was necessary for the company to survive with the help of a new, graphical way of using a personal computer.

In such a case, as Marshall Goldsmith observes, a leader needs "courage, humility, and discipline" to live up to the expectations placed on them. We, as coaches, are aware of the difficulties that both beginners and experienced leaders encounter at this stage.

> There is no perfection, only beautiful versions of brokenness.
>
> —Shannon L. Alder

Mindset and self-awareness will always remain the key issues when working on your change management skills. It is your maturity and the above-mentioned leadership qualities that will determine not only the success of implementing a given change but also whether you will see your team members when you look back.

What is often seen among leaders should be avoided: the blind pursuit of perfection at any cost. What distinguishes great leaders is the ability to be here and now, self-awareness at every stage of the road or stage of change—and, above all, the ability to spread it to others. No change is final, so there is no need to try to perfect its final form. What matters is your consistent work on it based on small, consistent steps.

People are said to fear change. In fact, people fear the pace of change. They are afraid that they will not be able to adapt to the new conditions in time and that they will suffer some loss. A humble and courageous leader recognizes this fear and is the one who will focus on the horizon with attention and calm, standing among his people and for them.

> Change is avalanching upon our heads and most people are grotesquely unprepared to cope with it.
>
> —Alvin Toffler, *Future Shock* (2017)

If accepting the change is the first step, then embracing it is the next. Apart from the pace of change, employees and even leaders often struggle with a lack of faith in the effectiveness and purposefulness of a change. The reasons for the lack of faith in change are usually very individual and result from previous experiences, including relationships with superiors, upbringings, and many others.

Earl Nightingale (n.d.) proposed his idea of setting goals. His intentions were pure, as he claimed, "People with goals succeed because they know where they are going." At first, the entire Western world went crazy about this idea. It quickly penetrated industry, becoming one of the basic tools for monitoring progress and strategic planning. The idea took root deeply and passed on to the next generation, entering the labor market.

The triumph of the idea of goal setting is something to celebrate, from the industrial arena to everyday life. With time, it became common to set not only professional but also private goals: another house, a better car, a beach house, a new lover. As time passed, however, the idea became distorted. Extremely high goals were replaced by unrealistic goals, impossible to meet, and the awareness of managers began to penetrate the conviction that the most important thing was to explain why "it did not work out this year," to safely preserve their job positions.

And here we come to the heart of the problem. Setting goals has become synonymous with something that can and should be chased without exaggeration or without determination.

This is why communicating the need for change by leaders so often results in apathy, or even open aversion. If you ask a lot of employees, you will hear that they have bad memories of such endeavors. If you delve deeper, as a rule, it turns out that the most difficult stage for them was enduring the transition period. Without the supervisor's support and being present, new ideas and change are more difficult. This is how these bad memories about change are formed.

> Everyone thinks of changing the world, but no one thinks of changing himself.
>
> —Leo Tolstoy

IQ: What is the smallest possible immediate change of behavior as a leader for you? What would that mean for your employees?

Working on your own leadership skills should be a prelude to any major change in your team or company. It is also extremely beneficial from the point of view of inspiring and attracting members of your team to undertake the next long-term effort. As you work on yourself and change, you increase the chances that others will take risks to follow you. Modeling is still the number one teacher.

> It is not the critic who counts; not the man who points out how the strong man stumbles, or where the doer of deeds could have done them better. The credit belongs to the man who is actually in the arena, whose face is marred by dust and sweat and blood; who strives valiantly; who errs, who comes short again and again, because there is no effort without error and shortcoming; but does actually strive to do the deeds; who knows great enthusiasms, the great devotions; who spends himself in a worthy cause; who at the best knows in the end the triumph of high achievement, and who at the worst, if he fails, at least fails while daring greatly, so that his place shall never be with those cold and timid souls who neither know victory nor defeat.
>
> —Theodore Roosevelt, speech at the Sorbonne, Paris, April 23, 1910

IQ: Are you willing to be in the arena?

REFERENCES

Bridges, W. (1991). *Managing transitions: Making the most of change.* New York: Addison-Wesley.

Clark, K. (1998). *Life is change, growth is optional.* St. Paul, MN: CEP Publications (Center for Executive Planning, Inc.).

Coffey, C., & Lam, D. (2015). *The new IQ: Leading up, down, and across using innovative questions.* Reston, VA: Prism LTD.

Dannemiller, K. D., & Jacobs, R. W. (1992). Changing the way organizations change: A revolution of common sense. *Journal of Applied Behavioral Science, 28*(4), 480–498.

Earl Nightingale Quotes. (n.d.). BrainyQuote.com. Retrieved January 22, 2023, from https://www.brainyquote.com/quotes/earl_nightingale_383343.

Goldsmith, M. (2007). *What got you here won't get you there.* New York: Hachette Books.

Hord, S. M., & Sommers, W. A. (2007). *Leading professional learning communities: Voices from research and practice.* Thousand Oaks, CA: Corwin.

Johansen, B. (2007). *Get there early.* San Francisco: Berrett-Kohler.

Roosevelt, T. (1910). "Citizenship in a republic." Speech at the Sorbonne, Paris, April 23, 1910. *The works of Theodore Roosevelt,* vol. 13, pp. 506–529.

Toffler, A. (1970). *Future shock.* New York: Random House.

Tolstoy, L. (1900). *Pamphlets.* Christchurch: Free Age Press.

SECTION I

The "WHY"

Lots of people begin by telling us what they do or how they do it. Simon Sinek wrote a book called *Start with Why* (2009). I (Bill), when preparing people for interviews, start with "Why do you do this work?" The "why" describes a person's purpose as a professional and in life. It reveals the passion that exists for the work they choose to do.

Every day we get challenged in our jobs and positions to make decisions that someone else thought would be good. When those problems and decisions are aligned with our "why," it becomes an easier fit. When not aligned, internal and external struggle can occur.

> "Walking your why" is the art of living by your own personal set of values.
>
> —Susan David, *Emotional Agility*

Chapter 2

Some Basics of Leadership

This chapter discusses a few of the organizing principles that create a culture in which people want to work. After all, if the culture is not right, star performers will be able to find another job. One of the best fringes an employer can offer is an engaging, collaborative culture.

> Put an excellent leader in a school and its teaching force soon follows—whether the school is private, public, or charter. The inverse is just as true. Yet for two decades, our education debate about tenure, charter, and vouchers has drawn our attention from the first-order issue of reimagining school.
>
> —Ted Dintersmith, *What Schools Could Be* (2018)

Just as Dintersmith explains the power of leadership in schools, you will find the same in business. What attracts and retains your best people, their networks, and their ideas? Employees are the source of learning that keeps both schools and companies competitive—mainly competitive with themselves. The enemy is not out there. It is in us.

> Leaders choose to teach. And teaching is an inherently humble act—focusing first and foremost on the development of others.
>
> —Richard Sheridan (2018), Menlo Innovations

Thirty years ago, serving as a high school principal, I (Bill) refused to let a student drop his chemistry course. The student responded by saying he would just stop attending classes. That would mean that we would have a different conversation, I countered. Then I offered to tutor him. A week later, he showed up at my office door, asking whether my offer was serious. We worked on his assignment for about thirty minutes, and, as he was leaving, the student turned back to say, "You should have been a teacher." This was one of the best compliments I had ever received from a student. It was an "aha" moment. Kids sometimes think principals become leaders without any connection to the classroom. Though I had been a math and physics teacher, I wasn't as good at chemistry as I had once been. I did manage to remember that a mole was not only a furry animal but also a measure of concentration of solute in solution. Either way, that student made my day.

Sheridan is right: as a leader or presenter, standing in front of thirty or more moving targets is humbling. And as we said in the last chapter, humility is an important attribute. It helps to let your employees know that you are willing to walk in their shoes, sweaty palms and all.

Jakub Grządzielski has led others in various positions for nearly two decades. While still a student, he encountered the works of Dale Carnegie. In particular, he and his future leadership were impressed by the book *How to Win Friends and Influence People*, in which Carnegie teaches that it is worthwhile to look for what others are better at than you are. No leader accomplishes goals alone. Build a team with skilled people that support the challenges of other team members.

Think about how this strategy will perfectly position you as a leader. By adopting an attitude characterized by respect and appreciation of the skills of another person, you create endless opportunities for cooperation and mutual trust. In today's transparent business world, the ability to build relationships and build your own personal brand based on the opinions of other people is indispensable.

> Leadership is social influence. Leading Schools [and businesses] require multiple leaders.
>
> —James Spillane (2006)

In *The Leadership Engine* (1997), Noel Tichy and Eli Cohen summarize the two main responsibilities of leaders: (1) to be the head learner, and (2) to develop other leaders. As new leaders, we often do not think we are responsible for developing other leaders. To be a leader, you must learn and develop others. It's almost as though, subconsciously, each of us accepts that most senior managers are obliged to educate new leaders, including potential successors. But we still do not understand the essence of this process. That is why, in your environment, you may meet with a fear of transferring experience and know-how or even find that less gifted people are being promoted because they are seen as submissive and dependent on their promoters. However, if you turn the page over and look at it as an opportunity to support and surround yourself with highly competent people, you will gain great opportunities to benefit from their growth and be seen as an excellent coach.

> Our leaders and aspiring leaders must be active learners. We must continually adapt or will we also disappear.
>
> —Richard Sheridan

> In the long run, the only sustainable source of competitive advantage is your organization's ability to learn faster than your competition.
>
> —Peter Senge (quoted in Sheridan, 2013)

So, how do we keep learning? Reading, attending conferences, and technology can help us surround ourselves with other learners. They sometimes provide perspectives unavailable to us when we see only through our own eyes. More diversity of perspectives leads to better decisions. Look inside the organization first: Who are your learning omnivores? Who seems to be getting results when others say something cannot be done? First, mine the minds of those in close proximity to you. Then extend outward, bringing in more ideas. If you are actively looking for information, your contribution to the development of people and of the organization can take place on many levels. You can even start in the role of a scout, bringing new ideas or potential development directions and then considering their possible application.

Leadership based on fear can get short-term compliance. However, this does not work in the long term. This type of management style is nothing more than an emotional drain, impossible to bear by employees in the long run, resulting in low motivation levels and provoking aggression toward people from outside or a given interest group. Knowledge workers do not respond well to threats and intimidation. Psychological safety is required for the best thinking.

> The greatest competitive advantage in our modern economy is a positive and engaged brain.
>
> —Shawn Achor (quoted in Sheridan, 2018)

Leaders are critically important. Developing leadership in the organization will reap benefits. So, first, build a leadership team. In *The Four Obsessions of an Extraordinary Executive*, Patrick Lencioni (2002) encourages us to make sure that we get as many voices in the room as possible, especially those that we trust but do not necessarily agree with. Encourage employees to question the status quo. This is where the greatest resistance lies. Asking open-ended questions breaks down barriers to perceiving opportunities. Trust is the most important thing, because leaders need honest, differing points of view. John Gardner's (1990) *On Leadership* observes that we should "pity the poor leader that has unfriendly critics and uncritical friends." Never forget that wisdom.

Lencioni also encourages leaders to strive for organizational clarity. Diversity in the workforce can introduce novel answers to questions, provide new clarity of thinking, and add some creative ways to interpret problems. Given a chance, people will offer valuable thoughts *if* we ask the right questions. To adapt Ford's slogan, "Learning Is Job #1." If you are able to ensure fairness and integrity, placing a bet on diversity yields completely new possibilities and completely different points of view. This is what constitutes real wealth in today's world.

Next, Lencioni tells us to overcommunicate. We must keep talking about learning, writing about learning, and promoting learning to colleagues and community. People forget or get distracted. Leaders should strive to become the reliable source of information for your team. If, over time, your attitude is seen to be credible, and if you avoid filtering information, the natural need to look for sources of information will be satisfied, and all the energy of the team will be focused on the right track.

Finally, Lencioni suggests reinforcing leadership by aligning human systems to the goals of the organization. Are the systems in place reinforcing your goals, or are they working against learning and collaboration? Look at the feedback businesses are seeking in their companies. If you want someone to accept something, it must be an added value for them, not an artificial creation. This also applies to management styles. What often hampers a team's harmonious connection with the goals of the organization is the misconception of their superiors that the chosen direction of solutions should depend on them. It would be a better idea to create the right company culture and involve the team or teams in this process.

> Leadership is action, not position.
>
> —Harold "Bud" Boughton.

> Never mistake motion for action.
>
> —Ernest Hemingway

What stops us from taking action? Pfeffer and Sutton (2000) point to what they call the knowing-doing gap.

- *When talk substitutes for action:* Talk might feel good, but it will not lead to doing something positive. Try something, and if it works, keep doing it. If it doesn't work, try something else. As Richard Sheridan

says, "run the experiment." See what happens. You may experience procrastination and feel worse about yourself as time goes on. The most difficult moment is usually the beginning. Managing your calendar based on your job satisfaction at the end of the day can help to tip the balance in this case.
- *When memory substitutes for thinking:* Sometimes we have fears from the past, worries that the future will bring the same results, and we are having feelings in the present. Consider the possibility that what didn't work in the past, or what parts didn't work, may work now. Times change, people change, and the world is changing. The same applies to coaching. Coaching only refers to the past when there are experiences of which you can build your new direction or point of view, in order to start making changes.
- *When fear prevents acting on knowledge:* Fear can freeze people, preventing them from taking positive steps. W. Edwards Deming said years ago that we must drive fear out of the organization. Your organization is getting 100 percent congruence with what it is designed to do. If you want different results, look at the design of the organization and quit blaming people. In one of his TEDx speeches, Simon Sinek defined the target situation as one in which each employee would not have the slightest fear to raise a hand and say, "I need help" or "I have made mistake," knowing that the others will come to offer help.
- *When measurement obstructs good judgment:* Trust the judgment of those who are closest to the issue. They have the best view of what is working and not working. Remember that someone who works there eight hours a day not only knows what is working properly, and what is not, but also knows best what needs to be done or what needs to happen to change the state for the better. Relationships and relevance always trump regurgitation.

How do we overcome this "knowing-doing gap"? Here are a few ways:

- Be clear about why we are doing things the way we do. Are we getting the results we want?
- Find out what is working and do more of it. Have real meetings focused on learning, where the dialogue and exchange of ideas add to the repertoire rather than expecting a silver bullet, which simply doesn't exist for everyone.
- Try something. See what happens. Then adjust or try something else. Ask for feedback on what is working.
- If you don't want to make mistakes, you are probably not interested in learning. Fear of making a mistake will stop some really good ideas.

- Take fear, guilt, and shame out of learning. None of these three facilitate the learning process.
- Beware of false analogies. Fight the competition, not each other. Confirmation bias and attribution error are deadly to learning.
- Measure what makes the most sense. Content acquisition is probably not the best indicator of learning. Being agile is going to pay off in the long run.
- Where do leaders spend their time—the "Killer Bs" (budgets, boundaries, and bosses) or the "Lively Ls" (learning, leading, and lasting relationships)?

REFERENCES

Dintersmith, T. (2018). *What school could be: Insights and inspiration from teachers across America.* Princeton, NJ: Princeton University Press.

Gardner, J. W. (1990). *On leadership.* New York: Free Press.

Lencioni, P. (2000). *The four obsessions of an extraordinary executive: A leadership fable.* New York: Jossey-Bass.

Pfeffer, J., & Sutton, R. I. (2000). *The knowing-doing gap: How smart companies turn knowledge into action.* Cambridge, MA: Harvard Business School Press.

Sheridan, R. (2018). *Chief joy officer: How great leaders elevate human energy and eliminate fear.* New York: Portfolio.

Sheridan, R. (2013). *Joy, Inc.: How we built a workplace people love.* New York: Portfolio.

Sinek, S. (2009). *Start with why.* New York: Penguin.

Spillane, J. P. (2006). *Distributed leadership.* New York: Jossey-Bass.

Tichy, N. M., & Cohen, E. B. (1997). *The leadership engine: How winning companies build leaders at every level.* New York: Harper Business.

SECTION II

The "HOW"

You can start with your "why," but you must have the knowledge, skills, and applications of *how* to go about getting to that goal. The "how" is the process we use to accomplish our goals. It frames our thinking by providing positive actions we believe will help individuals and organization be successful. The "how" brings your "why" to action.

> You have to talk about your WHY and prove it with WHAT you do.
> —Simon Sinek

Chapter 3

The Seven Cs of Learning Cultures

You know what it is like when the best plans do not result in the outcomes desired. This chapter will provide seven specific areas with suggestions to help close the gap between existing and desired states.

Leaders must model learning and share leadership with staff where possible. Of course, leaders have a role and responsibility for safety, budgets, and staffing. However, nothing burns out staff members faster than working their tails off and not seeing results. "Learned helplessness" sets in, and the status quo wins. Organizations with high team cultures are more effective. Some of the ways to deal with such a difficult situation is to break the goal into smaller ones and then entrust them to employees in accordance with the agreed development directions. The condition is that they are *willing* to assume this role on the part of individuals. With a great commitment of support, not control, from their superiors, they achieve great success. This is mainly because the priority is people and their development, not the numbers themselves.

Creating a culture that will maximize learning for our students and maximize their creativity and talents is critically important. Creating the conditions for staff to share repertoire is a way to scale up individual pockets of excellence. As Eleanor Drago-Severson and Jessica Blum-DeStefano (2016) point out in their book, *Tell Me So I Can Hear You*, leadership can focus on helping professionals move to a self-transforming level where the whole system benefits. Keep the intellectual talent curious and provide momentum for solving tough problems.

The following are some current frameworks developed over the years. Many of the skills below overlap and can be used in multiple situations.

> Knowledge is important AND insufficient.
>
> —William Sommers (2019)

Let the confirmation of this thesis be, for example, the fact that in the 1930s, when Hitler began to climb to power and Nazism began to spread in more and more circles, German society at that time was probably the most educated society in the history of mankind. Mere education, knowledge, or intelligence is not enough in itself.

It could be assumed if you are reading this book that you want to add ways of increasing learning in your organization. Doing so requires the courage to address issues honestly, the humility to learn from multiple sources, and the willingness to follow through, as identified in chapter 1. Keep in mind that as you begin to delve into a variety of topics related to this book, new questions will arise over time as you begin to realize things that you simply didn't know or hadn't thought about before. If you decide to follow the answers to your questions, over time you will start to create and shape the reality in your management style, team, or organization.

Getting the culture right will be critical before working directly on the three Cs of productivity: cultural responsiveness, coaching tools, and community outreach.

1. *Communication* is key for all leaders and stakeholders, both internal (within the organization) and external (customers/clients and community)

> The medium is the message.
>
> —Marshall McLuhan

How do you communicate the weekly announcements and newsletters?

Some of the ideas to try are adding to the list of meetings. I (Bill) would disseminate weekly information to my staff with the title "Rational Inquirer." It started with a quote for reflection, included a list of meetings or updates on a project, offered some humor, and ended with a story for the heart. Feedback from staff indicated that it changed some of the conversations in the lounge, at the watercoolers, and in the hallways. Note that each of us has a communication need embedded in our DNA. It is through communication that you can express concern for another person, offer words of support, provide inspiration, or spark ordinary human curiosity. It is an essential tool for true leaders.

Write community newsletters including current book summaries, tips for parents/colleagues, and highlight employees that are doing creative things. Short book summaries have led to community members asking for additional information. Parent workshops can include topics like the Goldilocks theory of parenting, conflict management strategies, brain research, and so on.

Direct reports connect on the latest trends and updates. Attendance builds as people talk about these sessions. Also keep in mind that many people working within organizations are parents. They don't leave their families at the doorstep when they come to work.

In business organizations, learning events can be useful for customers both internal and external. This approach communicates the reciprocity of learning that enhances relationships and knowledge.

2. *Collaboration*: Leaders work with multiple groups of various sizes

Facilitation skills are necessary to get the most out of the time invested. Getting good ideas from talented and committed knowledge workers accelerates organizational learning. Bringing groups together with a common purpose is essential to be laser focused on learning. When working with various teams, it is worth paying attention to ensuring fair opportunities to influence the final result as well as the shape of a given project or product. Active listening and spending as much time as possible listening actively will, in turn, help identify potential sources of conflict.

Leading effective meetings that do not waste time is essential. Does staff look for ways to avoid coming to meetings or count the ceiling tiles during the meeting? Run a good meeting and people will come. Are staff meetings learning events or a series of information that could easily be done via email? What do people talk about at staff meetings? Learning and creative ideas, we hope. There will never be enough time or money to do everything we would like. Remember, however, that people will appreciate your meeting skills more if you make every effort to give space to all participants without letting those with greater charisma dominate. An attitude based on respect, curiosity, and the ability to ask good, open questions will make your meetings anticipated and considered effective by everyone.

Menlo Innovations, Richard Sheridan's company, has *the* best meetings. In "Hey Menlo" meetings, forty-plus people gather in a circle and share what they are working on, what they are learning, and where they could use some help. Twenty minutes later, after everyone has reported, people seek out those who can help. Learning transfers at a high rate and moves the system along.

> If your job is waking up the dead, get up, today's a workday.
>
> —Angeles Arrien

When a group forms, an activity on values created by Stan Slap (2010) can accelerate group cohesion. Slap makes a list of values and asks participants what their top five are. Then he has them cut it to three. The second question is the most important: How did they get those values? Sharing with the group builds trust and makes connections more possible. Beginning this way helps people make connections that are strong and meaningful.

A Trainer's Companion by Olsen and Sommers (2013) has stories that can be used to tee up learning activities. There are stories, quotes, and reflective questions in five categories: reframing, diversity, conflict, balance, and change.

3. *Coaching*: We consider coaching the highest possible form of people management

However, several necessary conditions must be met for this to be possible. Leaders must have a skill set including a continuum of conversational strategies from open reflection, coaching for excellence, evaluating, and, while not used very often, moving ineffective people out of the organization. A variety of protocols helps to have the right conversation at the right time. What are your best conversational skills?

One source we recommend is *Nine Professional Conversations to Change Our Schools: A Dashboard of Options* (Sommers & Zimmerman, 2018; see figure 3.1). These strategies are collected from education and business models.

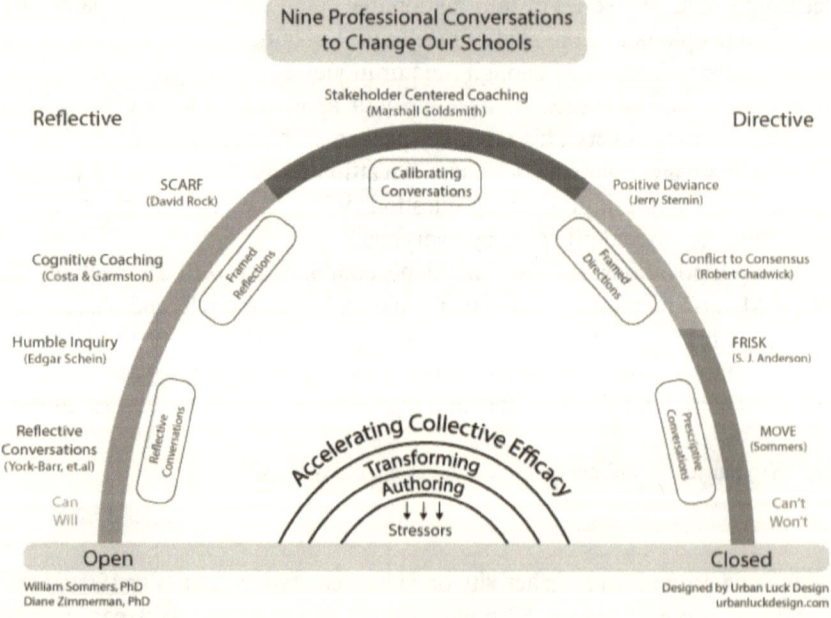

Figure 3.1 (*Source:* Sommers and Zimmerman [2018])

The dashboard starts with open reflection, then moves to other models that are more data driven, and finally (although rarely used) more directive. All of these have their place to increase development. See Drago-Severson and Blum-DeStefano's (2016) work for an adult development organizer. She has growth edge questions in her book that are powerful in helping educators continue to grow and learn.

Management through coaching is also possible in industry. Moreover, it is extremely effective. Why? Again, because it is geared toward people and their needs. As coaches, many times during a session we meet with the statement that such a situation is not possible due to the extremely complicated specificity of production processes. There should be additional charges for something like this: if you accept the fact that people can decide or give an opinion on how a given process takes place when they want to influence its shape and efficiency, then you will agree that every leader, regardless of the industry, should have their employees in the center of attention, not the process itself.

> People need different approaches. Choose wisely.

It is extremely important that leaders have a repertoire to meet the varied stages of adult teacher development. Coaching focuses on development not deficit. Supervisors can always move to deficit and power if needed. We try to change the behavior before enforcing more restrictive measures.

4. *Conflict*: Working with kids, colleagues, organizations, and community often results in conflict

Leaders who are at the sites deal with conflict from direct reports and those the leader reports to in the organization. Having smart people who don't necessarily agree with one another can be the best learning situation, or the worst nightmare.

In my (Bill's) 2019 book, I collected more than thirty conflict management strategies for individual and group situations that provide a repertoire of responses depending on the issues. A friend once asked me why, several years ago, I had twenty-five strategies. I responded, "I had twenty-four and none of them worked." I suggest acquiring as many conflict management strategies as possible. I am currently at thirty, looking for number thirty-one.

What strategies have been most effective for you? Which ones have not worked? Which ones are the most effective in what kind of situation? How are you acquiring more conflict management strategies? We may not like conflict *and* as a leader, you will have to deal with it. Make it a positive, if possible, rather than wasting emotional energy. If you really do not want to deal with conflict, we suggest you find another occupation.

You also need to be aware of how much depends on your executive presence and communication when different views clash. Look at the situation in such a way that the debaters chose to participate, putting their reputation or inner peace at risk to directly help you make the right decision—your behavior should express a high form of gratitude and appreciation for this effort.

5. *Change*: Having skills to manage change reduces the anxiety for leaders and those who depend on leadership; managing change effectively reduces the energy spent on the unknown and helps keep the focus on learning

Anyone who thinks things will go back to "the good old days" is not paying attention or lives in a different universe. In fact, some of the good old days weren't that good. Charters, online learning, and governmental decisions continue to affect our schools and funding. You can see the results even more in industry. What you can do about it is harmonize your self-awareness with the progressive change in such a way that you begin to see it as your journey and feel excitement instead of anxiety or nervousness. There is a huge difference between excitement for what is ahead of you and your team, and uncertainty or fear. Note that the first attitude already includes a positive acceptance of change.

Globalization, technology, and speed will continue to drive change for the foreseeable future. How are you managing change? What processes do you use when helping others through change while keeping the focus on learning?

Three effective strategies for managing change include:

- Richard Beckhard's model—D x V x F > R = C—*dissatisfaction* times *vision* times *first steps* must be greater than *resistance* to equal *change* (cited in Dannemiller & Jacobs, 1992). Look back at page 3 for a more complete description.
- Mary Lippitt (2003) has a model of "managing complex change" that we think is very powerful and can foreshadow problems. Using this technique as a quick check may save you lots of time by making sure all the elements are present before starting a new initiative.
- Suzanne Bailey taught a model called the "gameboard of change." This is a great process for walking through the multiple stages of change. Knowing the barriers and creating solutions ahead of the change can be very productive and time effective while including more people.

6. *Creativity*: The best organizations keep thinking creatively about what works, what doesn't, and what to try next

Creativity is the lifeblood of a system and helps the growing diversity of learners be more successful. Change will require creativity. Change = learning, learning = change.

Creativity takes a completely different level when passion appears in what you do. This is when we say that work is no longer a job but a life mission. Then you create to change the reality around you in the way you think is right and you strive to leave a permanent mark. There is always curiosity behind creativity. Curiosity about people, the world, phenomena, processes, or new directions of activities, in turn, means openness and acceptance of something new and unknown.

> We can't solve problems by using the same kind of thinking we used when we created them.
>
> —Albert Einstein

> The people with the most flexibility will have the greatest influence.
>
> —Bob Garmston

What we, the authors of this book, have collectively learned in forty years of being learners and leaders is "if it isn't working, try something else." It is that easy and that hard.

> One way to be more creative is "changing perspectives." When getting ideas from someone outside the organization, someone from a different position inside education (students/employees included), or someone with diverse perspectives, better decisions are made and are more inclusive of multiple points of view.
>
> —Edward O. Wilson, biologist, *Diversity of Life*

Wilson said, "All living systems, whether plant or animal, benefit from diversity." Diversity can provide stability. We have found that diversity usually generates alternatives and provides options that may not be readily apparent without seeking feedback from others. With alternatives and a variety of options, as a leader, you can make assumptions that support and define your decision. However, the condition for their formation is, similarly to ecosystems, ensuring diversity. The disturbance of this balance and the loss of this valuable stability usually means the withdrawal of some factors, resources in favor of those who will fill this place or even dominate or replace it.

7. *Courage*: Leadership is not for the faint of heart; speaking truth to power, managing up, having strong values, and making timely and tough decisions are at the heart of leadership

Choosing the "right fight" is critical in developing people and systems.

There are courageous leaders out there. Dr. Dennis Peterson, superintendent of Minnetonka Public Schools in Minnetonka, Minnesota, was asked, "How do you decide who to hire as a principal?" Dr. Peterson responded, "If they cannot have the hard conversation, they can't work for me." Do you have strategies to do "hard things"?

Courage in a leader also relates to his integrity, regardless of whether his actions coincide with what he communicates or whether his behavior changes during uncomfortable situations. You should be aware of this, and it is in such situations that your people will watch you especially closely and make decisions about whether to trust you and follow you.

Developing the skills of stating your opinion without the emotional load is important. Emotions are strong motivators, positive and negative. People can react to style rather than substance. So, pick the right issue.

Courageous leadership is also, and perhaps above all else, a readiness to take up difficult and unpopular topics or problems. We don't mean to imply that everything is a fight. Not that standing up for something or trying to please everyone is not always a good strategy. Sometimes conflict is seen as a fight between positions. Leaders cannot fight (or deal with resistance) over every issue. To help determine whether the time and energy are worthwhile, we suggest looking at *The Right Fight* by Joni and Beyer (2010), who offer six "right fight" principles:

- *Make it worth fighting about.* Make it material. Make the stakes big enough to motivate people.
- *Focus on creating the future.* Right fights are not about the past.
- *Pursuing noble purpose.* Go beyond self-interest.
- *Make it sport, not war.* There should be rules and rules shouldn't change during the conflict.
- *Structure right fights.* Work informally with people you have relationships with. Bob Chadwick has a very good consensus model. (See Sommers and Zimmerman's *Nine Professional Conversations* for the specific strategy.)

- *Turn pain into gain.* Pain can energize people. When there is an issue and leaders manage it correctly, the struggle can create trust, collaboration, and increase the interdependence of the culture. Everyone who participates benefits from the outcome, even the possible losers.

Also note that being courageous and not being afraid to exchange views is not a bad thing. On the contrary, if you separate emotions from the essence of the matter and do not allow them to influence your judgment, it will enable you to learn about different, often unknown experiences, opinions, and, above all, inspirations. The world is not black and white. It consists of many shades. Therefore, sometimes a minimal change of optics is enough to get inspired or to inspire other people around you. Without this form of courage and awareness of how much you can influence the world around you, it will be difficult for you to be seen as someone you want to follow.

Courage was not the absence of fear, but the triumph over it.

—Jim Hightower

It is imperative that leaders find people who they trust and who don't necessarily agree with them. Ask them for their opinion. If you go ahead with a plan or decision, even though professionals might disagree, at least you have thought through possible adverse consequences. More diversity of opinions helps make better decisions because we consider more points of view.

REFERENCES

Dannemiller, K. D., & Jacobs, R. W. (1992). Changing the way organizations change: A revolution of common sense. *The Journal of Applied Behavioral Science, 28*(4), 480–498.
Drago-Severson, E., & Blum-DeStefano, J. (2016). *Tell me so I can hear you.* Cambridge, MA: Harvard Education Press.
Gardner, J. (1990). *On leadership.* New York: The Free Press, Inc.
Joni, S., & Beyer, D. (2010). *The right fight.* New York: HarperCollins.
Lencioni, P. (2002). *The four obsessions of an extraordinary executive.* San Francisco: Jossey-Bass.
Lippitt, M. (2003). Leading complex change. Article published by Management Enterprises Ltd.
Olsen, W., & Sommers, W. (2013). *A trainer's companion: Stories to stimulate reflection, conversation and action.* Baytown, TX: AhaProcess, Inc.
Slap, S. (2010). *Bury my heart at conference room B.* New York: Penguin.

Sommers, W., & Zimmerman, D. (2018). *Nine professional conversations to change schools: A dashboard of options.* Thousand Oaks, CA: Corwin Press.

Tichy, N. M., & Cohen, E. B. (1997). *The leadership engine: How winning companies build leaders at every level.* New York: Harper Business.

Wilson, E. O. (1992). *The diversity of life.* Cambridge, MA: Belknap Press.

Chapter 4

Communication

Communication is key for all leaders and stakeholders, both internal (within the organization) and external (customers/clients and community). How the message is delivered is as important as the content of the message. Remember Marshall McLuhan and his seminal work, *The Medium Is the Message* (1967)? How do you communicate the weekly announcements and newsletters?

Some of the things we have tried or have seen done with weekly announcements is adding them to the list of meetings. We call ours the "Rational Inquirer." Staff have told us it has changed some of the conversations in the lounge and in the hallways. (See below for a description.)

Note that each of us has a communication need embedded in our DNA. It is through communication that you can express concern for another person, offer words of support, provide inspiration, or spark ordinary human curiosity. It is an essential tool for true leaders.

Write community newsletters including current book summaries, tips for parents/colleagues, and highlights of employees that are doing creative things. We have had community members ask for additional information based on the short summaries of a book we provided. We have hosted parent workshops on topics like the Goldilocks theory of parenting, conflict management strategies, brain research, and so on. Attendance builds as people talk about these sessions. People in organizations are often parents.

Weekly bulletins are another form of internal communication:

- The format starts with a reflective saying, a poster, or proverb with a few questions to answer.
- Then include announcements for meetings, organizational information, and/or upcoming events.
- Next, include some humor (always appropriate, of course).
- Finally, end with a story for the heart—something that deepens the culture, collaboration, and caring.

For education, it is extremely important to keep the parent community aware of potential changes in policies, results, and community outreach. When writing or making videos or external communications for community, suppliers, or customers, think of adding value to their issues. This becomes an extra service to them. They appreciate it.

As Patrick Lencioni (2002) says, "Overcommunicate organizational clarity." We can't overcommunicate. People forget or sometimes ignore unless they hear the same message multiple times. John Livesay (2022) writes in his book that the "sale is in the tale." People remember stories more often than descriptive text or tables of data. What is your story? How will you increase impact with stories, proverbs, and metaphors? Here are a few sources to get you started:

- Walter Olsen and William Sommers, *A Trainer's Companion* (2002)
- Anne Wilson Schaef, *Native Wisdom for White Minds* (1995)
- William Sommers, "New Rules" and "Book Summaries" (available at www.learningomnivores.com)

Here are some of our favorite proverbs:

- French: Children need models more than critics.
- Chinese: It is easier to stay out than get out.
- Yiddish: Beware of the prophet who carries only one book.
- African: Not learning is bad; not wanting to learn is worse.

Another strategy to get your message across is video clips. Commercials, videos that teach, and videos you see on the internet can be great sources. One we use a lot is *Be Open Minded*, from PBS. Watch it and use it to tee up conversations about initial stereotypes; then, at the end, the context changes.

Here are a few tips to consider:

- Acronyms can help retain knowledge.
- Stories and videos that provoke emotion will increase retention.
- Ask one thing—this is your call to action. Get a commitment for one new idea.
- Follow-up—this is the assessment and helps determine the discipline to complete an action.

REFERENCES

Lencioni, P. (2002). *The four obsessions of an extraordinary executive*. San Francisco: Jossey-Bass.
Livesay, J. (2022). *The sale is in the tale*. Los Angeles: Tradecraft Books.
Schaef, A. W. (1995). *Native wisdom for White minds*. New York: Ballantine.

Chapter 5

Facilitating Collaboration

> If you look at the way we meet in organizations and communities across the country you see a lot of presenters, a lot of podiums, and a lot of passive audiences. This reflects our naiveté in how to bring people together.
>
> —Peter Block, *Flawless Consulting* (2011)

Working effectively with multiple groups—whether grade level, departments, site councils, student leadership, or parents—requires skilled facilitation. Whatever your position, even if you are working alone, collaborating with others is a foundational skill. Whether or not you are interacting with one person in a face-to-face meeting, a small group with specific goals, or a large group developing implementation strategies for a company vision, the way in which a leader facilitates meetings can make a difference in whether people attend and/or contribute during those meeting. Using time wisely is critical to getting good ideas from talented and committed people.

Most research indicates that meetings are the biggest time wasters in organizations. Let's look first at facilitation skills and how they can contribute to a meeting's effectiveness.

How #1: We highly recommend the book *Flawless Consulting* by Peter Block (2011). He is a master at facilitating groups to get positive outcomes. Peter's strategy for transferring knowledge, skills, and applications involves finding two other people you don't know well, sitting with your knees six inches apart, and discussing the question(s) that have been asked. The result is that participants expand their own perspectives from the point of view of colleagues.

How #2: How does a convener make sure that the meeting has an agenda and specific parts for interaction resulting in a plan to move forward? Dick and Emily Axelrod (2014), in a book titled *Let's Stop Meeting Like This*, suggest six steps to running good meetings. They use the metaphor of being in a canoe.

Meeting Canoe

1. *Welcome*. Sometimes a quick check-in is helpful. This gets everyone's voice in the room.
2. *Connect*. Why are we here? What is the person's connection to this group or issue?
3. *Discover*. What is the current state of affairs? Take an assessment of the way things are.
4. *Elicit*. What do we want? Creating a vision of what is a desired outcome provides a goal statement.
5. *Decide*. What can we do? Developing action steps provides guidance for making progress. It becomes your action plan. Vision without action is only a dream.
6. *Attend*. Make sure there is engagement until the end. Otherwise, people tend to leave the meeting early.

We will add one more point to the Axelrods' process. After developing actions, outline what the evidence of progress will be, in both the short term and the long term. Or agree to KPIs (key performance indicators) or metrics to track progress. When the group meets again, start with this question: What have we seen or heard that says we are moving closer to our outcome?

How #3: Depending on the ability and willingness of the group(s) a leader is working with, there are many strategies to use published in my (Bill's) book *Creating Talent Density* (2021). Here, I provide twenty-five ways to work with groups to develop talent in ways that bring out the best in everyone. It offers guidance on assessing the ability and willingness of a school's faculty and staff.

First, decide the level of expertise and engagement of the group. Michael Ayers and William Sommers (2020) adapted "situational leadership" by Paul Hersey. See figure 5.1.

Below is a list of frameworks and coaching strategies that, depending on the diagnosis of the group, can create cultures in which sharing ideas is the goal.

> Prescription without diagnosis is malpractice.
>
> —James Muir

Low Ability, Low Motivation
- Chadwick Process
- Work on Relationships
- CHaD—Marshall Goldsmith

Figure 5.1 Situational Leadership (*Source*: Sommers [2021])

- Norms for Collaborative Work
- Covert Processes at Work

Low Ability, High Motivation
- Psychological Safety
- Pareto Principle
- Instructional Coaching
- Cognitive Coaching
- Positive Deviance Conversations

High Ability, Low Motivation
- SCARF
- Radical Candor
- Know Your Values, Share Your Story, and Build Trust
- Emotional Anorexia
- Joy, Inc.

High Ability, High Motivation
- Social Physics
- Multipliers
- Principles
- Culture Code
- Leveraging Polarities

Extended Learning Options for Your Learning Omnivores
- BrainTrust—used at Pixar
- Work Rules—used at Google
- Business Review Plan (BRP)—used at Ford and initiated by Alan Mulally
- Trillion Dollar Coach Process—Bill Campbell
- No Rules Rules—Netflix

Each of these specific strategies can be used to facilitate learning, distributing knowledge, and building trust within work groups. The reason there are several is that no one strategy will work every time and in every case. The flexibility to pivot when necessary increases the feeling of progress that aids in group communication and support.

Next, let's turn to the coaching/supervision model in the next chapter to support individual and group learning.

REFERENCES

Axelrod, D., & Axelrod, E. (2014). *Let's stop meeting like this.* Oakland, CA: Berrett-Kohler.
Block, P. (2011). *Flawless consulting* (3rd ed.). San Francisco: Jossey-Bass.
Sommers, W. (2021). *Creating talent density.* Lanham, MD: Rowman & Littlefield.

Chapter 6

Coaching and Supervision

Life must be understood backwards. But it must be lived forwards.

—Søren Kierkegaard

There is a continuum to be applied when supervising people. One of the tenets of special education is to begin with the least intrusive and restrictive process first. Then increase as needed to move toward more successful leadership. Figure 6.1 provides a dashboard of strategies and frameworks for supervisors and managers to reference with the goal of supporting, influencing, and intervening to increase performance.

The dashboard starts with open reflection, then to other models which are more data driven, and finally (although rarely used) more directive models. All of these have their place to increase development. Eleanor Drago-Severson

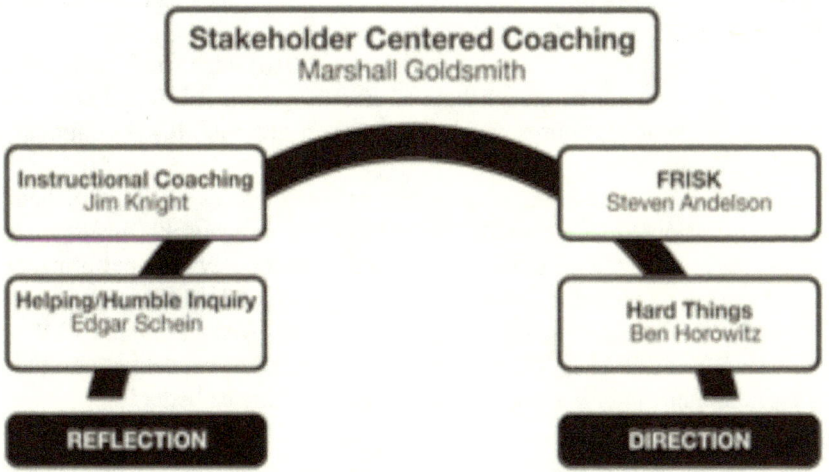

Figure 6.1 (Courtesy of Bill Sommers)

and Jessica Blum-DeStefano (2016) have written an entire book focused on how to give feedback that is based on adult learning and development growth. *Tell Me So I Can Hear You* includes growth edge questions that are powerful in helping educators continue to grow and learn.

Managers and leaders are always under time pressures. One of the most common obstacles to getting a coach, meeting with a coach, and having the discipline to follow through is lack of time. One goal for this book is STAR (save time—add repertoire).

By adding repertoire, leaders have more options, which builds competence and confidence in multiple situations. The one who has the most flexibility has the most influence in the current business and nonprofit environment. Adding a repertoire of skills with educational and business leaders will increase their influence in getting things done with cohorts.

An epistemological foundation for this chapter was presented in the 1980s by Charles Garfield (1987) in his book *Peak Performers*. The characteristic most identifiable with extraordinary people was an internal locus of control, also known as efficacy.

Julian Rotter, a psychologist, coined the term "locus of control" in 1954. It supports the research on personal and professional efficacy and agency. When people believe they can do something, they take more responsibility for solving the problems. In the context of coaching, the locus of control applies to the amount of control the coach/supervisor is willing to give to the client.

Another psychologist, Albert Bandura, defined self-efficacy as a person's belief in their ability to control their own life, well-being, and accomplishments. Part of self-efficacy is a consciousness of what interventions produced success. It is important for a coach/supervisor to believe that they have capacity to influence others toward desired outcomes; they can also validate efficacy through observation and feedback.

Efficacy requires reflection. John Hattie (2016) identified "collective efficacy" as the number one attribute of effective teams. He found an effect size of 1.54, which is four times the next closest attribute (0.4 is commonly accepted as significant).

In figure 6.1, on the left side, are more reflective processes. Edgar Schein, an organizational development expert from Massachusetts Institute of Technology, has written extensively on the subject of elevating performance for individuals and teams. Although we recommend all of his publications, two will start the conversation: *Helping* (2009) and *Humble Inquiry* (2013). As Peter Block (2011) says in a recent book, "[we] all owe a debt of gratitude to Edgar Schein and his work in helping organizations be better."

REFLECTION

Helping and *Humble Inquiry* by Edgar Schein

Helping (2009) by Schein provides some strategies to move a relationship forward. Help is only help if it is seen as help. We know from our experience that for help to be given, *and* accepted, the client and the coach must be willing to engage in the conversation. "Trust is a must" between the helper and the client.

Five possible traps for the client:

1. *Initial mistrust*: Will the helper be willing and able to help? Such caution is normal and appropriate but may cause the client to hide the real problem at first.
2. *Relief*: Having finally shared the problem with someone else who may be able to help, the client certainly feels relieved. Along with that often comes a welcome sense of dependency and subordination.
3. *Looking for attention, reassurance, and/or validation instead of help*.
4. *Resentment and defensiveness*: The client may look for opportunities to make the helper look inept.
5. *Stereotyping, unrealistic expectations, and transference of perceptions*: The client calibrates everything the helper does against these expectations and judges the quality of the growing relationship on this basis rather than on the help given.

Five possible traps for the helper:

1. Dispensing wisdom prematurely.
2. Meeting defensiveness with more pressure.
3. Accepting the problem and overreacting to the dependence.
4. Giving support and reassurance.
5. Resisting taking on the helper role.

The helper, coach, or supervisor can choose to be an expert who provides information, a doctor who will diagnose the problems and prescribe a solution, or a process consultant who will focus on the relationships and specify what kind of assistance will help. Below are some principles and tips to provide effective help:

- *Principle 1*: Effective help occurs when both giver and receiver are ready.
- *Principle 2*: Effective help occurs when the relationship is perceived to be equitable.

- *Principle 3*: Effective help occurs when the helper is in the proper helping role.
- *Principle 4*: Everything you say or do determines the future of the relationship.
- *Principle 5*: Effective helping starts with pure inquiry.
- *Principle 6*: It is the client who owns the problem.
- *Principle 7*: You never have all the answers.

Helping lays the groundwork for Schein's next book, *Humble Inquiry*, in which he focuses on questions rather than answers. How do we get the most ideas for possible solutions? Itzak Rabbi, Nobel Prize winner for physics, said one of the reasons he thinks he has been successful was because of his mother. When he came home from school, she didn't ask, "What did you learn in school today?" Instead, his mother asked him, "Izzy, what good questions did you ask in school today?" Dr. Rabbi said the focus of his responsibility was on asking questions and to be curious, the foundation of his own learning.

Not all questions are equivalent. Humble inquiry is the fine art of drawing someone out, by asking questions to which you do not already know the answer, of building a relationship based on curiosity and interest in the other person. What seems to help move thinking along is asking the right questions. To paraphrase Peter Drucker, the leader of the future won't necessarily know the answer. They will know the right questions. What a shift.

Humility is required for learning. Humility signals "I don't know but am curious to find out how or what others know." We suggest asking people with more experience to help us. Ask those who have already had successes. Those who are willing to learn from others can be the most productive conversations. Humility is one of the things we look for in Stakeholder Centered Coaching to find good people who want to be better. Think about it: if you already know everything, what's the point of a conversation?

Asking a question helps clarify what the other person wants. Schein relates the story in his book about his daughter coming down to his study to ask a question, to which he responded by saying she was interrupting his work. His daughter left crying. His wife came down and said his daughter just wanted to know whether he wanted a cup of coffee. All of us can probably relate to this story because we have done similar things—feeling guilty, making assumptions, and not clarifying the issue.

Here are some things Schein has learned from his experience:

- When the choice is between you or me, look for a way to explore us, the relationship itself.

- Ask an open question to get information that you need (a question that is not answerable with just a yes or no).
- When one is too busy with one's own agenda but wants to display a caring attitude, what often works best is a small change in behavior, not a total revision of the relationship.
- A small change allows a brief interruption to get more information before making a big decision.
- The small change should invite joint problem-solving.
- Small changes now avoid the need for big changes later.
- Humble inquiry would have enabled a small change.

Control the process (not the content) first. Content can follow and is enhanced when the process is right.

Here are some other learnings that are distributed throughout the book:

- Don't jump in telling answers until you know what the other person really needs to know.
- Don't assume that the person with the question has asked the right question.
- Asking for examples is not only one of the most powerful ways of showing curiosity, interest, and concern but also—and even more important—a way to clarify general statements.
- Accessing your ignorance, or allowing curiosity to lead you, is often the best guide to knowing what to ask about.

Much of Schein's work has great potential to enhance what is learned in meetings. Knowing that some meetings are not a safe place to ask questions, most people will complain about meetings. These sample questions can help mediate a couple of problems with meetings. Many times, there is encouragement to get into action before thinking.

Another problem with some meetings is "the culture of TELL." We meet, the person with positional authority tells all attendees what to do, and the meeting is ended. Most companies that are successful have safe meetings, exploring options and finding or developing creative solutions.

Schein ends with a series of questions that might be useful to get to the root of the problem:

- What is going on here?
- What would be the appropriate thing to do?
- What am I thinking and feeling and wanting?

If the task is to be accomplished effectively and safely, it will be especially important to answer the following questions to add to the knowledge and skill base:

- On whom am I dependent?
- Who is dependent on me?
- With whom do I need to build a relationship in order to improve communication?

Developing helping relationships is critical and using humble inquiry can lead to building trust and generating more ideas. Schein's third book, *Humble Consulting* (2016), relates how these tenets are applicable to being a consultant. Consultants, of course, can be external or internal.

Some of the major points made in his work *Humble Inquiry* include the following:

- Slow down and ask what is on the other person's mind.
- Ask questions that require explanations and expand the information flow.
- Use questions to expand options and resist the need to help.
- Reflect on how this inquiry expanded your knowledge of yourself and of others.

Management through coaching is also possible in industry. Moreover, it is extremely effective. Why? Again, because it is geared toward people and their needs. As a coach, many times during a session I hear the statement that such a situation is not possible due to the extremely complicated specificity of the production processes. There should be additional charges for something like this! If you accept the fact that people can decide or give an opinion on how a given process takes place when they want to influence its shape and efficiency, then you will agree that every leader, regardless of the industry, should have their employees in the center of attention, not the process itself.

Let's look briefly at a model developed by Jim Knight for instructional coaching of educators that is applicable to all leaders.

INSTRUCTIONAL COACHING

The Impact Cycle

The Impact Cycle process was developed out of years of coaching research (Knight, 2017). The three stages of the cycle can appear deceptively simple; however, to be performed well, they involve a sensitivity to the complexities of human interactions to support teachers staying engaged and hopeful about improving outcomes for students. The Impact Cycle involves three phases:

1. Identify
2. Learn
3. Improve

Throughout all three phases, the coach works to maintain a partnership relationship with the teacher that focuses on respect, collaboration, and reflection—not on control.

In the *identify* phase, the coach assists the teacher in doing three things:

- Getting a clear picture of the classroom reality. (What's really going on with the students in the area about which the teacher is concerned?)
- Setting a goal for student improvement in that area. (This is what we call a PEERS goal: a powerful, emotionally compelling, easy, reachable, student-focused goal.)
- Choosing an instructional strategy to help the students hit the goal.

During the *learn* phase, the coach helps the teacher to implement the instructional strategy that the teacher chose in the *identify* phase by:

- Clearly describing the strategy with the help of a one-page description and a checklist (see *Factor Four: Instructional Playbook* by Jim Knight at Instructional Coaching Group).
- Providing modeling of the strategy at the teacher's discretion and encouraging time for the teacher to practice the strategy.

The final phase, *improve*, involves the teacher implementing the strategy. The coach supports the teacher in whatever ways the teacher requests (including data collection, data analysis, troubleshooting concerns, etc.) to make any necessary adaptations until the goal is met. Topics of conversations that may occur during the *improve* phase include:

- Confirming direction
- Reviewing progress
- Inventing improvements
- Planning next actions

The Impact Cycle process ensures a focus on student growth, not on perceived teacher deficits. Its emphasis on student-focused goals means it is a process that can provide data to directly tie the work of the coach with the teacher to student progress.

Data

Effective instructional coaches are skilled in gathering data to help teachers set goals and to monitor progress on those goals. The teacher sees a clear difference between what their coaching looked like before their district instituted a program and what it looks like after a concerted focus on goal setting with teachers as the focus.

Before goals became the focus, Michelle would approach a teacher in the hallway and ask, "How are things going?" And typically the teacher would say, "Fine." When approaching another teacher, she would say, "How's using that new strategy going?" Again, she received a reply of "Fine." In approaching yet another teacher, she might try a different approach, asking, "Anything I can do to help you?" only to get the response, "No, thanks. I'm good." Despite Michelle's attempts to engage with teachers, not much deep conversation about classroom improvement happened because the conversations lacked focus.

Referring to specific goals changed the conversation. When Michelle asked, "What's the progress on your engagement goal?" she and the teacher had a deeper, more specific, and more helpful discussion.

STAKEHOLDER CENTERED COACHING (MARSHALL GOLDSMITH)

In 2007, Marshall Goldsmith wrote a book called *What Got You Here Won't Get You There*, focused on Stakeholder Centered Coaching. Stakeholder Centered Coaching is about improvement. As the environment and world changes, our knowledge, skills, and applications will have to keep pace. Why do people stay with what has been working and believe it will always produce good results? When the world changes, we might have to modify what we do to keep pace with changes. Marshall discusses strategies that will help leaders get feedback on what behaviors that are working and what are not, our barriers to behavioral change, and how "feedforward" can increase productive results.

Second Lesson: People don't get better without follow-up. Follow-up was defined as an interaction between would-be leaders and their colleagues to see whether they were improving their leadership effectiveness. Those who followed up made improvements. Those who didn't, didn't improve.

Third Lesson: There is an enormous disconnect between understanding and doing. Nobody ever changed for the better by going to a training session. They got better by doing what they learned in the program. Doing involves follow-up. Becoming better leaders is a process, not an event.

So, if you want a coach, what are some things to consider?

It shouldn't be a chore for your coach to get in touch with you. Making excuses won't make the process valuable.

1. Your coach should be interested in your life and have your best interest at heart. There are many people out there calling themselves coaches. Choose wisely.
2. Your coach asks questions about your goal. They are not there to judge you.
3. Pick an issue in your life that you're not happy with and that you want to improve. Make a list of daily tasks that will help you get to your goal.

Goldsmith coined the term "feedforward" for leaders and those who want to help the leader get better. It is focused on what you are going to do differently. There is nothing you can do about the past. There is an enormous opportunity about how you will behave differently ad for the better in the future.

Here is an example of the process of Stakeholder Centered Coaching:

- Goal(s)—interview leader
- Stakeholders—to determine the leader's stakeholders, answer the question "Who do you trust?"
- Interview stakeholders
- Coach creates themes and recommendations
- Leader chooses a goal(s)—pick one (or two)
- Coach checks with supervisor to insure an accurate goal
- Statement to stakeholders about goal(s) selected to be more effective
- Ask stakeholders for examples of progress or lack of progress by using mini surveys along the way
- Summative survey

FRISK

Steven Andelson (1998) wrote about a process to clarify goals and expectations for performance improvement. The acronym FRISK provides a memory hook to remember the steps. They are as follows:

F—Facts that provide evidence of the conduct
R—Rule that establishes the authority

I—Impact of the behavior on the work environment
S—Suggestions for improvement and statement of expectation
K—Knowledge of the employer's right to provide corrective action

It is important to realize FRISK is still an attempt to correct unproductive behavior. The goal is to keep the employee and make it clear what will be required to remain and contribute. This step is usually reserved for those who are having negative effects on others. See research from Will Felps on "bad apples" for further information.

A quote from Diane Zimmerman, PhD, and a former superintendent of schools: "Being nice did not work with this teacher, but being firm and clear did. I never had another problem."

Hard Things about Hard Things by Ben Horowitz

Occasionally, a decision must be made about separation. In my (Bill's) experience, there have been only four times in forty years when removing an employee was necessary. Jathan Janove (2017), in his book *Hard Won Wisdom*, calls this the cost of avoidance: "Employers tolerate problematic employees for years, never assessing the cost of keeping them employed." The cost can be financial, emotional with colleagues, and/or the community served. Janove uses the acronym of DISsing them: direct, immediate, and specific.

Ben Horowitz (2014) has a quote: "If you are going to eat s##t, don't nibble." Here are some of the salient points Horowitz suggests in a process:

1. Get your head right. Make sure you know what and why you are taking the action.
2. Don't delay. Avoidance will cause emotional stress for you and the employee.
3. Be clear about why you are taking the action.
4. Address the team or whole organizations that will be affected.
5. Show up and be visible.

Remember this saying attributed to many authors: "*What you permit, you promote.*"

It is extremely important that leaders have a repertoire to meet the varied stages of adult teacher and employee development. Coaching focuses on development, not deficit. Supervisors can always move to deficit and power if needed. We try to change the behavior before enforcing more restrictive measures.

People need different approaches. Choose wisely.

REFERENCES

Andelson, S. J. (1998). *FRISK documentation model.* Available at https://blogs.svvsd.org/administration/2014/09/14/using-the-frisk-documentation-model/.

Block, P. (2011). *Flawless consulting* (3rd ed.). San Francisco: Jossey-Bass.

Drago-Severson, E., & Blum-DeStefano, J. (2016). *Tell me so I can hear you.* Cambridge, MA: Harvard Education Press.

Garfield, C. (1986). *Peak performers.* New York: Avon Books.

Goldsmith, M. (2007). *What got you here won't get you there: How successful people become even more successful.* New York: Hyperion.

Hattie, John. (2012). *Visible learning for teachers.* New York: Routledge.

Horowitz, B. (2014). *The hard thing about hard things.* New York: HarperCollins.

Janove, J. (2017). *Hard won wisdom: True stories from the management trenches.* New York: Amacom.

Knight, J. (2017). *The impact cycle.* Washington, DC: Corwin.

Schein, E. (2009). *Helping: How to offer, give, and receive help.* Oakland, CA: Berrett-Koehler.

Schein, E. (2013). *Humble inquiry: The gentle art of asking instead of telling.* Oakland, CA: Berrett-Koehler.

Schein, E. (2016). *Humble consulting: How to provide real help faster.* Oakland, CA: Berrett-Koehler.

Søren Kierkegaard Quote. (n.d.). Quotespedia. Retrieved March 2, 2023, from https://www.quotespedia.org/authors/s/soren-kierkegaard/life-can-only-be-understood-backwards-but-it-must-be-lived-forwards-soren-kierkegaard/.

Chapter 7

Conflict and What You Can Do about It

If you are a person who leads executive teams, you'll surely admit that managing day-to-day issues, especially when many employees are operating remotely, is a demanding task. Because communications for remote employees are often via email or employee message systems, communication subtleties such as gestures and facial expressions are missing. Some believe that employees are less inhibited in online interactions than they are in face-to-face settings.

The present time is extremely demanding for those who lead others. We, in discussion with leaders, found that nearly 60 percent of executives say they spend time mediating human conflict. Therefore, we would like you to remember how your conflicts can be prevented, resolved, and managed. There are specific strategies that can positively affect working relationships.

Conflicts in interpersonal relations are common and inevitable. They happen even in the most harmonious of teams. What distinguishes great leaders, however, is the way they approach conflict management. Proper conflict management, based on the principles of leadership, will allow you to create stronger bonds within your team, encourage positive interpersonal relationships, and increase your ability to inspire your team. An additional benefit is the ability to generate the creativity and innovation necessary to lead others.

A conflict among team members can arise when there is a big difference in the assessment of the situation, which results in a rise in tension and associated emotions. A conflict can be accompanied by stress and the desire to stay with your own opinion as being the only correct one. Felps et al. (2006) write that "one bad apple" can reduce productivity up to 40 percent. What if there were multiple bad apples? The following strategies will help manage individuals, teams, and large groups.

SPEND TIME WITH PEOPLE AS A LEADER

As a leader, it is important to spend time with people. Being with your staff members is an excellent opportunity to identify potential sources of current and future conflict, giving you a chance to proactively manage it. Interaction with the team has a positive impact on team members, too, because they can share their doubts and concerns with leaders and hear answers to their questions. Listening also positively inhibits the development of conflicts. Lack of contact with others often causes misinformation to spread and causes frustration. Conflict between employees and groups can arise because of a lack of information, misinformation, and people making up negative scenarios.

The worst attitude that a leader can take when dealing with conflicts in a team is to avoid dealing with the problem. Leadership best practices tell us that leaders are responsible for the working conditions and atmosphere in the team.

Avoidance ends up being abdication. Without the intervention of a supervisor, difficult interpersonal workplace problems will not solve themselves; instead, they escalate and therefore cause greater losses to the team and/or the entire organization. Over time, a leader who does not respond to an existing conflict within the team risks loss of reputation among their team members.

If you properly manage your team, it means that you also care about the relationship between you and your team, as well as caring about mutual trust. And this is the foundation for resolving conflicts. When people believe the leaders have their direct reports' best interests in mind, parties to the conflict will want to cooperate honestly to end the conflict. The reason for this result is that people will be aware that it is not your goal to hurt any of them; rather, it is to stop the unfavorable situation before serious problems occur. It is not in our human nature to remain in conflict with others but to bring harmony and order to the group. Ray Dalio (2017), in his book *Principles*, says two elements are necessary to keep focused on the work rather than on negative relationships:

1. Radical transparency
2. Radical open-mindedness

Here are some of the foundations critical for building trust and managing conflict in the workplace.

LEADERS MUST REMAIN CALM AND OBJECTIVE IN THEIR ATTITUDE

When an obstacle arises during conflict, people will look at the leader and how they are reacting first. From my (Jakub's) experience, we advise that a leader should remain calm and objective in attitude and think carefully about how (as well as what) should be communicated. In conflict situations where negative emotions are flowing, the leader must not succumb to the negative atmosphere, instead guiding everyone through the conflict resolution process from beginning to end.

When starting the process, it is extremely important not to assume anything in advance and remain open to both sides. During conflict management, active listening is a particularly important trait that will allow you to gather additional information that will be key for taking adequate steps and to analyze the conflict fairly. It will also assure direct reports of your positive intentions. Stay focused so that you perceive a problem as specific behaviors. There is usually a set of circumstances and the outcomes that we want to avoid, which can contribute to negative feelings.

During the conflict management process and during simultaneous conversations with team members, the most effective tactic is to direct the conversation to the future and to possible ways out of the difficult situation. Even better, you should set a plan not only for resolving the current conflict but also for those that may arise in the future, regardless of what happened in the past.

CREATE A COMMON PLAN TO ADDRESS FUTURE CONFLICTS

To resolve interpersonal conflicts, parties must work together to find a solution that will satisfy these diverse interests. When individuals have a different work style or value system, there is a need to calmly discuss these differences and to create a common plan for the future with both sides. That is why it is so important to ensure that there are conditions that will help both sides to cooperate, which will also lessen the distance between them.

1. Polarity Partnerships

As an overall strategy, decide whether this is a problem to solve or a polarity to manage. A polarity exists when there are two good options and the best answer is not one or the other. To make this decision, consider whether the problem and boundaries are clear—if so, the issue is probably a problem.

Vignette 1 — Problem to Solve

A high school had 350 parking spaces for students. The parking permit requests by students numbered 750. Retro-fitting the baseball diamond for parking was considered as an option, but the costs eliminated this plan as a viable solution. Solution: The principal put 750 names in a hat and drew 350 names. Those names drawn got permits; those not drawn did not receive a permit to drive on campus. Outcome: 400 students and parents were upset. Sometimes a leader can't please everyone.

Vignette 2 — Polarity

Ten percent of a school's teachers were going to retire for the following year. That meant twelve to fifteen positions would be open. Question: Does the principal hire only veteran staff, or are newer, less experienced staff members hired? Use figure 7.1 to consider both possibilities. There are two good possibilities. To be a polarity, there are two requirements:

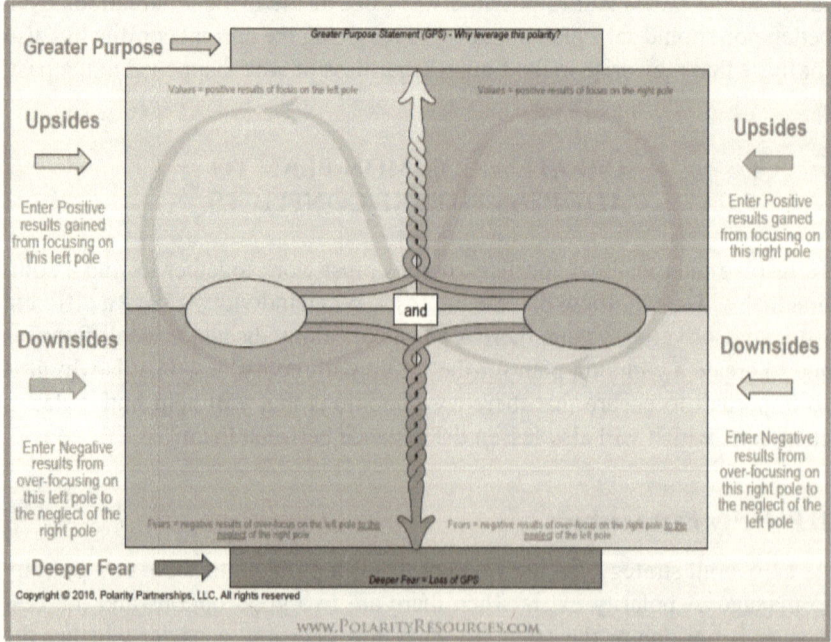

Figure 7.1 Greater Purpose Statement (*Source*: Copyright © 2016, Polarity Parnerships, LLC)

- Two polarities are interdependent. An example of interdependent is breathing. We need to inhale and exhale, content and context, individual and group.
- Two polarities are ongoing.

The ovals on each side might represent newer, less experienced staff on one side and veterans with experience on the other side. The upper-right quadrant shows the positives of hiring less experienced staff:

- more technology adept at new delivery systems
- willing to coach, advise, and support co-curricular activities
- more willing to try new strategies

The upper-left quadrant includes the positives of hiring veteran staff:

- experienced leadership
- long-term relationships with the community
- have experience with new ideas, both plusses and minuses

The lower- left quadrant includes concerns for hiring less experienced staff:

- sometimes too impulsive with new techniques
- can be seen as a threat to status quo (this might be an upper-left issue)
- less knowledge of community and resources

The lower right shows the concerns for hiring experienced staff:

- less willing to try new technology
- less willing to advise, coach, and so on
- might have outside alliances with community staff that could be difficult

If a polarity is interdependent and ongoing, solutions will be sustainable. Implementation accommodates both good ideas rather than choosing one or the other. As a leader, you must be active during these conversations and moderate them in a sustainable way. Being creative and unconventional in proposing possible solutions can be an answer. A post recently shared on LinkedIn was "Crazy Might Work." Remain objective in your assessment of the situation. As a leader, you are expected to lead and resolve the dispute in a positive manner.

When communicating to your team that the conflict has been resolved and that solutions have been developed, pay special attention to avoid making direct references to those involved in this situation. This will allow them to keep their reputation intact while avoiding the possibility of devaluing them in front of the team.

Nowadays, employees often have a problem with being heard by their colleagues and superiors. Therefore, you can often hear opinions and regrets about not being heard by others, as well as the fact that business leaders are often absent during vital conversations.

In recent years, organizations have started to emphasize the need to discuss, but the success of such activities depends primarily on the individual leaders who carry out these discussions. The lack of ability to actively listen by the supervisor may even make matters worse, as the employee will have their feelings confirmed that their voice has not been heard.

Go forward and manage conflicts for better productivity.

FOUNDATIONAL SKILLS

Accuracy—Probing for Specificity

- unspecified nouns and verbs
- universal quantifiers
- rules
- comparators

AAA—I Made a Mistake

- acknowledge
- apologize
- action

Admit that I don't know

The foundational skills start with probing for specificity to clarify the issue. If you cannot define the problem, you can't solve or manage it.

2. Accuracy—Probing for Specificity

When there is fuzzy language, fuzzy thinking occurs. Here are two examples.

Vignette 1

A teacher comes in to see the administrator and says, "The kids are coming late to my class." The administrator could go down to the classroom and lecture the students on being on time to class. However, another approach is for the administrator to ask the teacher, "Which kids, specifically, are coming late?" Most times the teacher will respond by providing the names of three students. Three students are different from thirty. The teacher and administrator might meet with three students as a group or individually. Lecturing the whole class usually results in resentment from those who are attending on time.

Vignette 2

A direct report complains to the supervisor that colleagues are not attending meetings on time. Option one might be to hold a staff meeting saying, "Some of you are not showing up on time for meetings." This approach usually lowers staff morale. Everyone in the meetings knows who isn't showing up on time. Result: Most people are mad at listening to blanket statements and believe the leader shows no courage for confronting those who are tardy to or missing meetings.

Solution: Who is consistently late or no-shows to meetings? Let's talk to them.

Figure 7.2 provides more examples of fuzzy language with possible responses. Get specific descriptions of the issue before jumping to solutions that may or may not be useful.

> A problem well defined is a problem half solved.
>
> —Charles F. Kettering

Our short version is "save time, first define."

Meta-Model/Specificity Model

Fuzzy Language	Getting Specific
Universal Qualifiers:	
all, everyone, never, forever, always	Has there ever been a time? Forever? Never? Everyone?
Modal Operators:	
should, must, necessary, can't, have to, ought	What stops you? Who made that rule? What would happen if you did?
Unspecified Verbs:	
prepare, make, think, do, feel, know, learn	Prepared how, specifically?
Unspecified Nouns:	
students, clients, women, they, people	Which administrators, specifically?
Comparators:	
better, larger, more profound, less useful	Better than what?

Adapted from Laborde, G. (1983). *Influencing with Integrity*. Syntony Publishing; **and** Bandler, R. & Grinder, J. (1979). *Frogs into Princes: Neuro linguistic programming*. Real People Press.

Figure 7.2 (*Source*: Adapted from LaBorde [1987])

3. AAA—Response, "I Made a Mistake"

No matter how smart an individual or group is, there are questions or consequences that we may not know. Also, there are knowns and not knowns. There are unknowns that are unknown. When presenting and/or leading, remember that people have great crap detectors. Don't try to sell an idea if it has too many unknowns. Most people have had smoke blown up their pant leg and are suspicious. Here is a short strategy that will increase trust whether the response is "I don't know" or "I made a mistake."

4. I Don't Know—Some Possible Responses

- What I do know is . . .
- I know who does know, and I will find out and get back to you.
- Does anyone else know? Or does someone have a suggestion where we can find out?

Honesty builds trust.

SMALL-GROUP STRATEGIES

Conflict to Consensus

- what are the issues?
- worst possible outcome
- best possible outcome—*goal*
- strategies and actions—*action plan*
- evidence—*assessment*
- follow up

Dealing with People You Can't Stand

- get it done
- get it right
- get along
- get appreciated

Strategies of the Dolphin

- sharks
- carps
- pseudo-enlightened carps
- dolphins

5. Affective versus Cognitive Conflict

- Affective is emotional and personal.
- Cognitive is data and research based.

Conflict is not always negative or something to deny. Amason et al. (1995) write about the difference between "affective conflict" and "cognitive conflict." The following are examples of affective conflict:

- Who does he think he is?
- Who made that stupid decision about . . . ?
- I think she just wants a promotion and will do anything . . .

These comments will damage relationships and increase triangulation (talking behind people's backs). I am mad at Sam, so I tell Sally he is a jerk. I don't deal with Sam directly. Not good.

Cognitive conflict, by contrast, can promote good decision-making and increase the feeling that comments are valuable and that everyone will be heard. These outcomes promote teaming and increase psychological safety, which Edmondson (2019) writes about. Cognitive conflict is putting ideas on the table, why the person believes this will help, and possible research that relates to the issue at hand. The more perspectives, the better the decision.

WHEN WORKING WITH INDIVIDUALS

Gottman's Successful Marriage
Managing Up
Emotional Blackmail

6. Gottman's Successful Marriage (adapted)

- anger
- complaint
- contempt
- silence
- separation

Vignette

After being assigned to participate on a new team, the group was not showing results. Two months together, and there were negative comments coming from team members. At the third month, one member of the team went to the supervisor. Yes, colleagues were starting to get involved, as the parents were complaining and colleagues were choosing sides. The principal scheduled substitutes for the classes and required a day-long meeting to deal with the conflict.

The principal taught the Gottman strategy to the team. The principal then asked each member where they would place themselves on the five stages. All stages were represented by the six-member team. There were tears and relief. The issues were on the table. Now they could be addressed.

All of issues were not successfully handled, but they were identified, and civility returned to the team. Students, as well as parents, were happy that the negative tone changed to neutral and there were some positive outcomes.

Result: At the end of the year, one quit teaching, one joined another team, and the rest reformed the team with agreements on collaboration commitments.

Steps to use for consensus building:

1. Get the stakeholders in the same room.
2. Create enough safety for the honest exchange of thoughts *and* feelings.
3. Show the five stages above and ask each participant where they are.
4. Ask: What is the worst outcome of not addressing these issues?
5. Ask: What would it take to make a more trusting collaborative team?
6. Agree on one or two actions steps.
7. Follow up: Reconvene in two weeks to check progress, whether positive or negative.
8. Recommit to the goal of trust and collaboration.
9. Follow up as many times as necessary.
10. The team will either move closer together or have insurmountable issues. If it is the latter, consider reassigning the team, or, in extreme cases, a colleague must exit.

7. Managing Up

Managing up is one of the top three issues that surfaces when coaching leaders. It will work regardless of whether the relationship with your supervisor is positive or negative. If it is negative, quoting Marshall Goldsmith, "If you can't sell an idea, if you can't change it, let it go." In this case, you can work with the relationship, do nothing, help the immediate supervisor get promoted, or find another position. Boss bashing has not proven to be an effective strategy, unless there are illegal or immoral issues. In that case, there should be data to work with.

The following process can be helpful.

- Good mouther—Spread positive messages about how your boss is effective.
- 5–15 plan—If being micromanaged, send a half- to full page of information each week including:
  a. positive accomplishments
  b. heads-up on issues that are on the horizon
  c. recommendations on how to handle future issues
  d. use bullets—your boss doesn't have time either; make it easy to read
- Liaisons—Make connections with those who have the supervisor's ear. Liaisons are positive triangles to help influence others.
- When nothing works—When you are considering leaving or are willing to go alone:
  a. Benign neglect—Just put orders aside and don't respond. What is being asked is not going to help you lead your team or will have negative impact on your leadership.
  b. Creative sabotage—Find or create other issues to help divert your supervisor's attention.
  c. Malicious obedience—Follow the directives to the letter. Doing so usually stops progress. You can't operate human systems by the contract. There are always issues that come up that don't fit a contract (one size fits all). Yes, we know contracts are important, but they will not solve every human conundrum.

8. Emotional Blackmail—Susan Forward

- Demand: a problem arises. Result: you deny or deflect.
- Pressure: a person applies pressure. Result: you deny or deflect.
- Threat: a person will go to your supervisor. Result: you deny or deflect.
- Two choices: give in or dig in.
  a. Giving in will get more of the unwanted or unhelpful decision with long-term consequences.
  b. Digging in will get your supervisor involved. Could be good, could be negative.

Vignette

A parent calls to get her son assigned to different teacher. You have just finished balancing classes, so each teacher has a similar number of students. (In this scenario, the principal knows that giving in to one parent could lead to others calling for the same reason.) The parent says, "We won't tell anyone." Pressure (TRAP). Principal says, "You won't have to; thirty students of the

Chapter 7

The Process

Figure 7.3 The Process of Emotional Blackmail (*Source*: Adapted from Forward [1997])

class your son leaves and the thirty students of the class he goes into will know." Sixty students and parents will immediately know about the change.

THREAT: Parents says, "If you don't, I will call the superintendent." (The parent happens to be a board of education member's spouse.) Decision point. Deal with one parent or deal with sixty. Hmmm, what do you think? Principal responds, "No, I will not change the teacher." Parent doesn't know that this change will cause another class to change. The two teachers teach at a different time.

OUTCOME: Parent calls superintendent. Superintendent calls the principal to ask for the change. Principal asks the superintendent, "How many calls do you want from parents for the same issue?" Superintendent says, "None." Principal says, "Get ready, because if you order me to do this, you will get more phone calls." Superintendent says, "I'll deal with this parent; don't make the change."

Memo to Principal: Consider long-term consequences before you make a short-term decision.

LARGE-GROUP STRATEGIES

There are times when the leader must present information or a vision and/or create energy among the organization's members. Sometimes there are responses from the large group that may show resistance or negative comments. The following are some behaviors that can help.

> How Not to Get Shot (not literally)
> Three Fs
> Sale Is in the Tale

9. How Not to Get Shot: Delivering Bad News?

- go visual
- off to the side
- eyes on data
- third person
- ninety degrees
- physically move
- reframe

Vignette

A principal was hired with the understanding that no financial issues were forthcoming. That was August. By January of the school year, cuts were being planned for the next year's budget. In February, the cuts were announced to the leadership team of each school. In an effort to explain to her staff before the rumors start, the principal called an emergency meeting with her school staff.

In the past, the meeting was held in the library. The principal always met with her back to the east wall. However, in this meeting she staked out her position so the staff would face the west wall. Locations have memories. She had prepared a PowerPoint presentation with two slides. Last year's staffing and budgetary information was on slide number two. When the staff entered, the first slide had a welcome message: "Thank you for coming on such short notice." The first words from the principal were "I have returned from the central office meeting concerning next year's budget. I want to share the information to reduce the change of rumors and the emotions of not knowing the real story on how our school will be affected" (Dalio's radical transparency).

- The information was visual as the second slide was revealed.
- The principal stood three paces to the left of the LCD.
- The principal looked at the slide and remained looking at the slide while presenting.
- The principal talked about "the staffing, the budget, the implications."
- The principal had her side toward the audience.
- Once the complete information was announced, the principal walked past the LCD, remained silent, and stopped three paces to the right side of the table.
- The principal turned toward the staff and said she would convene a meeting with team leaders the following day after school to deal with these budget concerns to determine the best way to proceed. As she reframed the conversation to how they would solve this issue, her hands pointed to the data and her body was openly toward the staff (high relationship).

She then posted the information in the staff lounge so everyone had access to the knowledge.

The next day, the leadership team met to start the process of how they would respond to the new budgetary data. Staff thanked her for being transparent with budget information, and for her courage in presenting immediately to the staff, and trust was maintained and increased.

10. Three Fs

- I *felt* that way . . .
- Now I *feel* this way . . .
- Because I *found* out . . .

Vignette

A superintendent was at a community meeting at one of the schools. A parent stood up and said, "I am tired of my child being in a class with so many special needs students. My child is getting short-changed by the teacher spending most of his time with special students. What are you going to do about this?"

The superintendent responded:

- "I *felt* that way once—that special needs students should be pulled out of regular classes."

- "Now I *feel* they should be mainstreamed as much as possible."
- "Because I *found* out that special needs students progress at a much higher rate when mainstreamed rather than being pulled out. The special needs students have more models for good behavior, regular education students benefit from helping special needs students, and society is full of diversity."

There were no more questions. The message was clear that the values of the school would be protected.

11. The Sale Is in the Tale

Words matter. Emotions and connections can be a great asset or a negative influence. John Livesay (2022) says, "Storytelling helps your career AND helps you make better emotional connections in your personal life, too!" Most people make decisions based on emotion rather than data only. Data is important but usually not the leading reason for decisions.

Most people want to hear why you are doing this work, not about the salary and fringe benefits. Organizations that pay attention to the culture will attract and retain team members at a higher rate than those who only pay more. One suggestion we have is taking improv classes. If you are going to do a lot of stand-up meetings, presenting, and public relations, improv strategies will be invaluable.

Here are some additional questions to consider:

- Have an elevator speech ready. Why do you do the work you do?
- Why did you choose this profession?
- Have stories about your organization. What worked, what didn't work, and what did you learn (case studies related to cross-cultural stories and metaphors)?

When dealing with potential conflict, managing it early is best. Leaders who cannot manage conflict will not survive very long or seal themselves away from problems. The goal is to manage conflict in order to spend more time on learning, creativity, and collaboration, not on firefighting. Remember, the more repertoire a leader possesses, the better able they are to choose a path forward.

REFERENCES

Amason, A. C., Thompson, K. R., Hochwarter, W. A., & Harrison, A. W. (1995). Conflict: An important dimension of successful management teams. *Organizational Dynamics, 24*(2), 20–34.

Dalio, R. (2017). *Principles: Life and work*. New York: Simon & Schuster.

Edmondson, A. (2019). *The fearless organization*. Hoboken, NJ: John Wiley & Sons.

Felps, W., Mitchell, T., & Byington, E. (2006). How, when, and why bad apples spoil the barrel: Negative group members and dysfunctional groups. *Research in Organizational Behavior, 27*, 175–222. 10.1016/S0191-3085(06)27005-9.

Forward, S. (1997). *Emotional blackmail: When the people in your life use fear, obligation, and guilt to manipulate you*. New York: HarperCollins.

Gottman, J. (1994). *Why marriages succeed or fail*. New York: Fireside.

LaBorde, G. Z. (1987). *Influencing with integrity: Management skills for communication and negotiation*. Palo Alto, CA: Syntony Publishing.

Livesay, J. (2022). *The sale is in the tale*. Los Angeles: Tradecraft Books.

Olsen, W., & Sommers, W. (2002). *A trainer's companion*. Baytown, TX: AHA Process.

Chapter 8

NAvigATiNg The rAPids of ChaNge

If you don't like change, you're going to like irrelevance even less.

—General Eric Shinseki

- People don't know what to do—lack of knowledge.
- People don't know how to do it—lack of skills.
- People don't know why they are doing something.
- People weren't involved in the decision-making.
- People are satisfied with the way things are.
- People say workload and pressure are increasing too fast.
- People can't see the benefits of changing.
- People don't see the change agent or advocate as credible.
- People don't sense support to implement changes required.
- People see that the innovation conflicts with school/organization culture.
- People are worried about failing.
- People have had negative experiences with change before.

Change is one of the reasons conflicts happen. We will address conflict more broadly in the next chapter. Michael Fullan (n.d.) lists many reasons "why people won't change."

One complaint educators hear is "those teachers won't change." Sometimes those complaints are correct. More often, the fact is that educators are changing all the time: new mandates, new politicians, new business requirements. The real issue is the delayed feedback loop. Business is normally on a quicker timeline. It takes a year or more to change curriculum or introduce new teaching strategies.

William Bridges (1991) writes, "Change is the game today, and organizations that can't deal with it effectively aren't likely to be around long." This situation affects both business and nonprofits. Change is the norm of life. Adaptability is—and will be—the survival strategy.

Before we introduce Richard Beckhard's model for change, we should first ask one question about the situation that concerns us: "Do people believe change is possible?" If the answer is "no," then reconsider whether the financial and emotional cost will be worth it. If there has been a history of false starts or a lack of long-term commitment to change, then people will resist changing. There is no long-term assurance the change will stick. Additionally, if there is a revolving door of supervisors, change probably won't stick. Superintendents of schools change about every three years, so many educators have consumed the hormone TTSP, commonly known as "this too shall pass." Wait it out. Because of this pervasive attitude, sometimes it is better to end and restart something new rather than change it. As a Chinese proverb notes, "It is easier to stay out than get out."

However, if people in the situation you are facing do believe change is possible, then it will be helpful to consider Beckhard's model of change.

There can be dissatisfaction, but without a vision of what the organization, supervisor, or individual wants, very few people will take the risk. And the next step is critical for leaders. The leader must orally and visually present the steps to get there. People need to see the goal *and* a pathway to accomplish that goal.

Once those three things—dissatisfaction, vision, and pathway—are greater than the resistance, change can happen.

Another change model that has been useful in our work is from Mary Lippitt (2003) at Enterprise Management. This model includes five steps and shows the results if any step is missing. Check figure 8.1 as it relates to previous change initiatives.

- Was there something missing?
- Did the result match the model?
- How would you have done this differently if you had considered this model first?

Our third change model provides a step-by-step process offered by John Kotter at Harvard, in *Our Iceberg Is Melting* (2005) and *The Sense of Urgency* (2008). In the latter book, Kotter addresses how to work with "No-Nos" (those who just don't want to change).

Managing Change

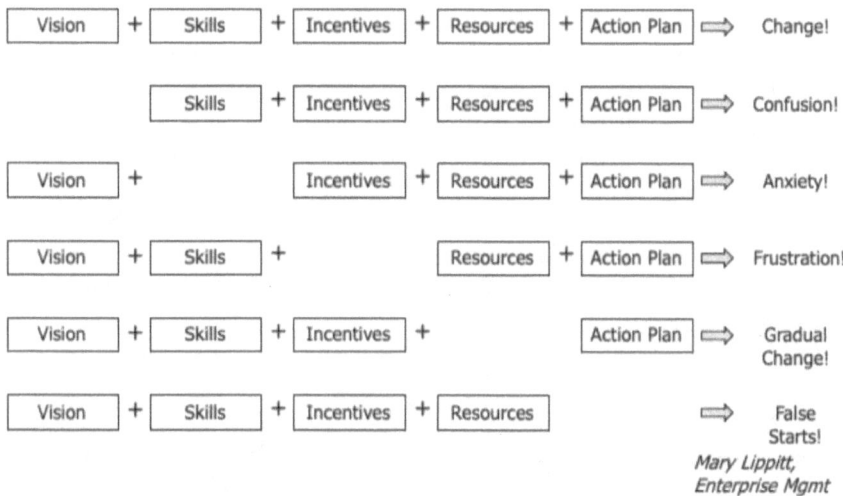

Figure 8.1 (*Source*: Adapted from Lippitt [2003])

> Our moral responsibility is not to stop the future, but to shape it . . . to channel our destiny in humane directions and to ease the trauma of transition.
>
> —Alvin Toffler

What you must also be aware of as a leader is the fact that change, especially in any industrial environment, is the third certainty (the first two you probably know: death and taxes). Constant changes are inscribed in the DNA of each production of solutions and products.

However, there is only one unknown: whether you will take part in change as a leader and supervisor, or as a spectator, alone and removed from the situation. Please remember, nature abhors a vacuum. If you don't undertake to guide your team through the challenges of change and progress, someone else will—even if it will be an informal leadership.

Therefore, it is up to you to choose whether you want to make a conscious decision. Take responsibility for the team and embark on this exciting, if sometimes difficult, journey—or not.

There is no right or wrong decision here that would meet our condemnation. You can either manage change and be seen as a true leader or remain a manager who only administers day-to-day affairs.

Looking at the required complexity in managing change, an interesting analogy immediately arises from the IT industry in multiple cloud storage systems. Cloud orchestration is the automated management of multiple workloads in multiple cloud solutions to aggregate them into one workflow. Thanks to orchestration, all elements of the IT infrastructure become one harmonious team that plays in accordance with our goals. This way we can see and manage it all at a very high level.

So, who and what can help you manage at a high enough level so that, on the one hand, you do not get stuck in operational tasks and, on the other hand, you have a real awareness of the challenges facing your team? The answer seems to suggest itself and is unequivocal: your coaching techniques are your version of cloud orchestration, allowing you and your team to work together effectively.

Coaching is also about providing support and guidance through various kinds of turbulence. For years, as indigenous cultures have taught us, we have lived in communities that needed leadership and the sense of security associated with it in return for better food or various privileges. As a society, we have always been able to sacrifice a lot for someone to help us live our lives in the best possible way. Despite the passage of years, this need has not died out—it is only insufficiently articulated in the mass media. We can even boldly assume that this need has been significantly strengthened over the last two decades as a result of changes in the pace of life, ways of doing business, or a significant reduction in the life of products.

So, are you ready? That is, *do you want* to lead your team through changes? The organization will move through the changes. The question is, do you want to be part of leading the change or be a bystander?

REFERENCES

Beckhard, R. (1969). *Organization development: Strategies and models.* Reading, MA: Addison-Wesley.

Bridges, W. (1991). *Managing transitions—making the most of change.* New York: Addison-Wesley.

Fullan, M. (n.d.) Resistance to change: Reasons and strategies. University of Vermont. https://www.uvm.edu/~cdci/best/pbswebsite/Presentations/ReluctancetoChange.pdf.

Kotter, J. P. (1996.) *Leading change.* Cambridge, MA: Harvard Business School Press.

Kotter, J. (2005). *Our iceberg is melting.* New York: St. Martin's Press.

Kotter, J. (2008). *A sense of urgency.* Boston: Harvard Business Press.

Lippitt, M. (2003). Managing complex change. Article published by Management Enterprises Ltd.

Chapter 9

Creativity

If you always do what you did, you always get what you got.

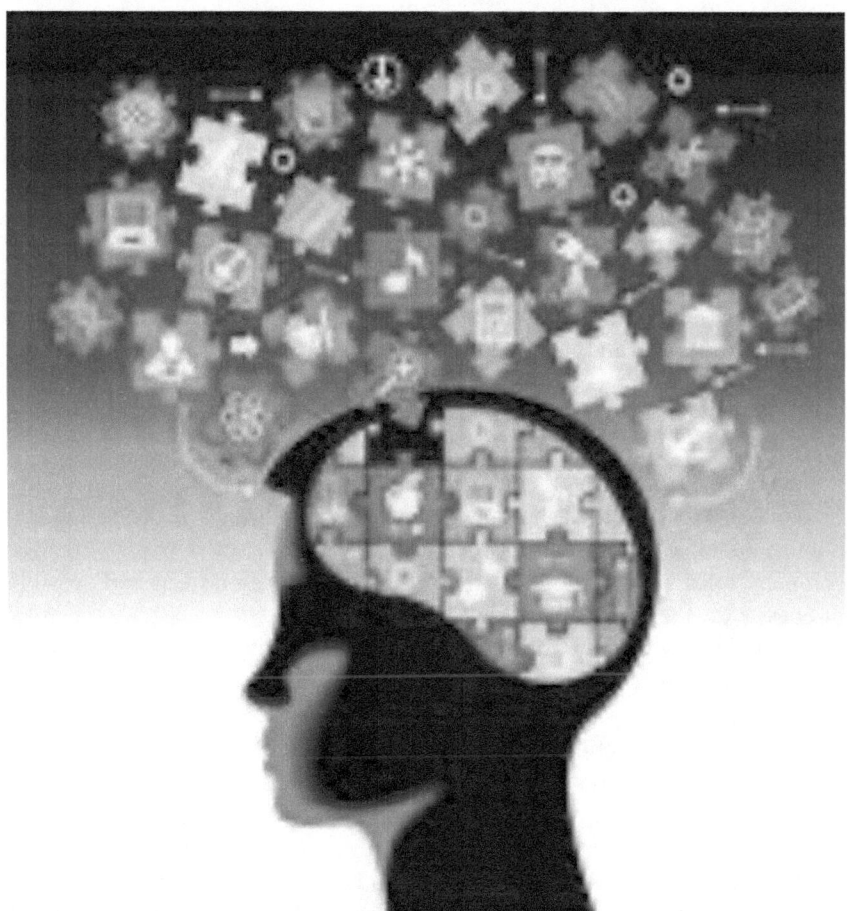

Figure 9.1 Creativity (*Source*: Internet download)

> Imagination is more important than knowledge. Knowledge is limited. Imagination encircles the world.
>
> —Albert Einstein

Several chapters of this book are behind you. You probably had the opportunity to close it during this time and think about your goals. What would you like yourself, your company, or your team to look like after you start working on your leadership skills and start influencing the development of your employees?

Surely you have already begun to recognize certain patterns of behavior, some negative and some positive, from the point of view of a true leader. There is another chapter ahead of you—this time devoted to creativity.

It will probably come as no surprise to the reader that the manager is not the center of attention here as an exceptionally creative creature, but instead the focus will consistently be on the team.

Creativity here is thought of as not only the ability to generate a certain number of ideas but also an element that unites, integrates, and builds the identity of the team. The "side effect" of this approach will be unfettered suggestions and a free flow of ideas from individual members of the team and the team as an interdependent whole.

In my managerial practice, I (Jakub) emphasized supporting my team and putting their creativity above my own ideas. I followed this practice in the creation of the department's vision for the coming years as well as during internal workshops and meetings. My role, however, was not limited to the skillful asking of open questions, active listening, and exploring the information obtained. In that case, my role would have been limited to that of a moderator.

Each day I spent seven out of my eight hours at work talking to my employees. Most often, these conversations were informal and concerned any number of topics, from current local events, changes, or new plans for the company's growth to—yes, you guessed it—optimization ideas and possible directions for the department's development.

Thanks to this way of working, I cultivated curiosity, my head filled with questions, doubts, or desires to change something for the better. The natural consequence was then to assemble the team, create optimal and safe conditions within the functioning team culture, and ask them these questions, stimulating their creativity. Importantly, I practiced this way for years, thanks to which my team members had an almost daily opportunity to train and strengthen their creativity.

The benefits of this approach were enormous. Creativity, inscribed permanently as an element of cooperation, was constantly developing in individual team members, providing unconventional solutions, building a sense of belonging to a group, and a sense of self-fulfillment. The effect of co-decision with co-responsibility quickly appeared, which, in turn, resulted in the fact that an idea was treated as their own from its inception to its implementation.

Another important consequence was the disappearance of unhealthy competition. Everyone had the opportunity to propose and implement solutions as they gained new professional experience, thus building better and better versions of themselves. So, there was no element of competition that was replaced by work in the chosen, individual rhythm.

Invaluable from the very beginning was the exchange of information and learning from each other. Open and ethical communication was particularly beneficial in stimulating creativity, clarifying solutions, and avoiding potential threats.

Let us now contrast such experiences with the kind of creativity favored by an "outstanding individual with unlimited knowledge." Surely you could name at least a few managers working in this way right now.

To visualize it now, please forget about all the benefits you read above, putting individual team members in the role of a contractor, where the only imposed goal is to deliver the commissioned task.

It could be unproductive. Fortunately, you have a choice.

PRE-WORK

Here are some strategies teams might use to prepare for sessions that will require creativity leading to innovation.

1. Word Ball

This is a warm-up activity taken from improv classes.

a. Get in a circle of four to eight people.
b. One person steps forward and, using an underhand motion, tosses an imaginary ball to another while saying a word of their choice: "carrot." (Any word will do.)
c. Whomever the person tossed the ball to now catches it, saying the first thing that comes to their mind—"orange"—as they toss the ball to a third person. There is no correct answer since the purpose is to generate possibilities without judgment.
d. The third person might say, "fruit," and toss to another person.
e. Continue for two to three minutes, going as quickly as possible.

f. Three to four rounds loosen people up, and many times the quantity of ideas increases.

2. Stroop Test

Colors are written in a font of a different hue (see figure 9.2). Each person reads the word, not the color. This helps close out previous thoughts and get ready to concentrate on a different topic.

red	green	blue	yellow	blue
red	blue	red	yellow	red
green	yellow	yellow	green	red
blue	yellow	green	blue	yellow
green	green	red	blue	green
blue	blue	yellow	blue	red

Figure 9.2 Stroop Test Example (Originated by John Ridley Stroop, American psychologist)

3. "Yes, and . . ."

This is another strategy from improv. Arrange people in pairs. Offer a prompt, like "plan your best vacation." One person might say, "I want to go skiing." Their partner responds, "*Yes*, that is a good idea, *and* we could stop at a beach on the way." The first person affirms the suggestion and adds another element: "We will stop at a beach, *yes, and* we can look for unique hotels to stay at." This exchange continues for four to five minutes. The goal is to expand the other's idea without negating it—to improve, not judge.

The following are some important concepts in Ed Catmull's (2014) *Creativity, Inc.* Ed was the president of Pixar, which produces well-known and beloved movies.

- Advanced Research Projects Agency (ARPA): "When faced with a challenge, get smarter."
- Ideas come from people. People are more important than ideas.
- A hallmark of a healthy creative culture is that its people feel free to share ideas, opinions, and criticisms. Lack of candor ultimately leads to dysfunctional environments.
- The overplanners just take longer to be wrong.
- Change is going to happen, whether we like it or not.
- The past should be our teacher, not our master.
- Groups often hold so tightly to plans and past practices that they are not open to seeing what is changing in front of them.
- Give a good idea to a mediocre team, and they will screw it up. Give a mediocre idea to a great team, and they will either fix it or come up with something better. If you get the team right, chances are that they'll get the ideas right.

These elements might be helpful to review before starting a project, when the energy has started to wane, and/or teaming must be re-established.

THOUGHTFUEL

In every crisis there is an opportunity.

Gary Klein (1998) studied firefighters, operating room teams, and EMTs, seeking to understand what thinking helped during high-pressure situations. He found that creative adaptable people have two main skills:

1. *Mental simulation.* This is *not* mental stimulation. We get a lot of that just living, leading, and contributing. Discussing scenarios prior to crisis or an unknown can help do reflection-*in*-action.
2. *Pattern recognition.* Knowing how processes should go or understanding what goes into a good practice helps a person know when there is a deviation. Klein tells a story about a fire chief who was directing a crew. He noticed a deviation. He pulled all firefighters out of the building. A few minutes later, the building collapsed. On reflection, the chief said, "Something just wasn't right." His experience saved lives.

Here is an activity to help understand pattern recognition (answers are at the end of the chapter):

- AEFHIKLMNTVWXYZ—What do these letters represent?

- ABCDEFGHIJKL?—What is the next letter after "L"?
- OTTFFSSENT—What might this series of letters represent?
- 0,1,1,2,3,5,8,13,21,34—Math and science people might do better on this one. What is the pattern? What is the next number?

John Kotter (2005) wrote *Our Iceberg Is Melting*. This metaphor reflects what is happening in most of the world and across most industries. The foundation is shifting under our feet. You may be standing on ice, and that iceberg is indeed melting. This is why creativity and adapting to a changing environment is so important. Few businesses, schools, and nonprofits will survive without planning a preferred future.

Figure 9.3 lists a few of the tenets that John Kotter (2005) presents in his book.

> A ship is safe in harbor, but that's not what ships are for.
>
> —John Shedd (1928)

Ian Mitroff (1997), in *Smart Thinking for Crazy Times*, offers the following answers to the question "Why do we have to change?"

- John Dewey: Western society is obsessed with the "quest for certainty."

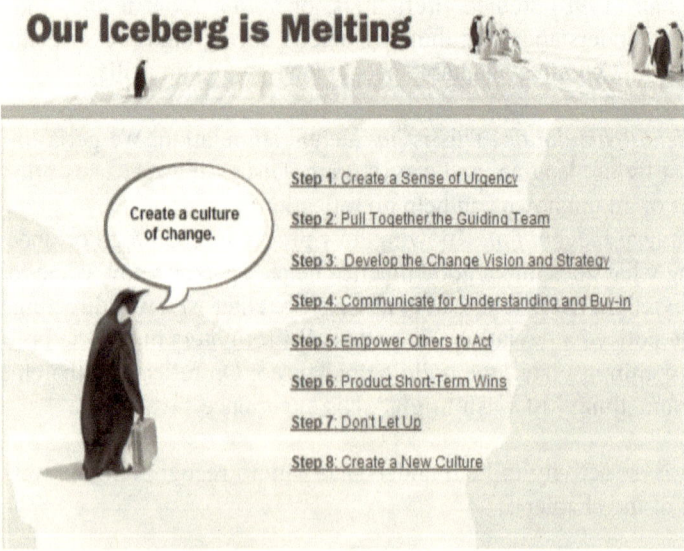

Figure 9.3 (Source: Kotter [2005])

- "What good does it do to find the best arrangement of the deck chairs on the *Titanic* as it is about to go down?"
- Walter Lippman: "To every human problem there is a solution that is simple, neat and *wrong*."
- Peter Drucker: "Nothing fails so much as overwhelming success."

It is important to validate opinions and theories. Checking for the following types of errors will save time and chasing wrong assumptions:

- Type I errors: false positives (you think the answer is right, but it is not)
- Type II errors: false negatives (you think the answer is wrong, but it is not)

How do we create moments that will be remembered for a lifetime? Dan and Chip Heath (2017) wrote *The Power of Moments*. Here are some of the elements to consider:

- What if a teacher could design a lesson that students remember twenty-five years later?
- Every great service company is a master of service recovery.
- Researchers at the University of Pennsylvania: "Bad Is Stronger Than Good."
- The secret to growing a business is to "reduce negative variance and increase positive variance." We want to keep doing what is showing good results and stop doing what ideas are not working.
- You can't appreciate the solution until you appreciate the problem.
- Action leads to insight more often than insight leads to action.
- In forty-six years of research, only one factor was cited every time as among the top two motivators: "full appreciation of work done."

This last point is reminiscent of a T-shirt design that read, "Underestimate Me; That'll Be Fun."

Answers from pattern recognition exercise above:

1. The capital letters are written with straight lines (no curved capital letters)
2. "O"—pattern is one vowel, three consonants, one vowel, three consonants, and so on
3. One, two, three, four, five, six . . .
4. The Fibonacci sequence (found on many math tests)

REFERENCES

Catmull, E. (2014). *Creativity, Inc*. New York: Random House.
Heath, C., & Heath, D. (2017). *The power of moments*. New York: Simon & Schuster.
Klein, G. (1998). *Sources of power: How people make decisions*. Cambridge, MA: MIT Press.
Kotter, J. (2005). *Our iceberg is melting*. New York: St. Martin's Press.
Mitroff, I. (1997). *Smart thinking for crazy times*. San Francisco: Berrett-Koehler.
Shedd, J. A. (1928). *Salt from my attic*. Portland, ME: Mosher Press.
Stroop, J. R. (1935). Studies of interference in serial verbal reactions. *Journal of Experimental Psychology, 18*(6), 643–62.

Chapter 10

Courage

Leadership is not for the faint of heart; brave leaders face challenges head-on.

—Susan Lucia Annunzio, president and CEO
of the Center for High Performance

Vignette

Michael and I (Bill) were colleagues as teachers in the 1970s and as high school principals in the 1990s. Michael has since passed away. As principals, we would meet every couple of months to share stories, frustrations, and ideas for solutions.

At one of our meetings, I asked Michael, "How do you keep your values intact when so many supervisors, parents, and community members want us to deviate from what is right for all kids?" Michael, whose ancestry is Native American, told the story of the "Suicide Spear."

There are times when, reflecting on difficult choices, a decision must be made. After a good night's sleep, go outside, and plant your spear in the ground. The leader has chosen to stand on this issue, at this time. The decision is, I am standing here, on this issue, and if you are going to kill me, kill me here—"I'm not moving."

This story has provided leaders with a metaphor for decisions about which issue is important enough to be "the hill you will die on." There is always a potential, for leaders, that this could be a career-limiting move. Remember, those who have the power to make a decision *can* make that decision. Make peace with that fact. At the same time, in leadership positions, the individual can think through what they are willing to get fired for. Think about this before an issue arises. Once in a difficult situation, you have no time to try to figure out where you will stand and show up.

Figure 10.1 The Suicide Spear (*Source*: Internet download)

I am always doing that which I cannot do, in order that I may learn how to do it.

—Pablo Picasso

Courage, humility, and discipline are required to elevate and sustain better leaders and the positive effects on organizations.

—Marshall Goldsmith

Another resource I highly recommend is Angeles Arrien's (1993) *The Four-Fold Way*. The four tenets in her work have provided a guide to help navigate through challenging leadership issues. Those tenets are:

1. Show up and be fully present.
2. Pay attention to what has heart and meaning.
3. Tell the truth without blame or judgment.
4. Be open to outcome, not attached to how to get there.

Leaders must demonstrate courage to be visible, focus on what is most important, be transparent with data and feedback, and help create pathways to accomplish goals for people.

Things that matter most should not be at the mercy
Of things that matter least

—Wolfgang Goethe

STORY OF ALICIO, THE MOST PROACTIVE MAN IN THE WORLD

Alicio works at a resort, taking guests out at night on the Amazon River. Angeles Arrien and Patrick O'Neill were staying at this resort and decided to go out at night to enjoy the river and be with other guests.

Alicio and a co-worker took several guests out in the boat at night. It was very dark because there are no streetlights on the Amazon River. Alicio, who was in the front of the boat, kept shining a searchlight out ahead of them. When asked what he was looking for, Alicio responded, "Two red dots." People didn't understand but trusted Alicio as they made their way down the Amazon River.

Finally, as the light shone on the bank of the river, two red dots appeared. The co-worker shut the motor off, and Alicio jumped over the side of the boat. In amazement, the tourists watched Alicio. *Splash, splash, splash.* They could barely see his silhouette, and then he was gone. All of a sudden, the people heard noises and rustling in the brush on the bank. "We hope Alicio is okay," said one person.

Splash, splash, splash. The hope was that it was Alicio. Soon the tourists could see his silhouette. He had something under his arm. As Alicio approached the boat, they could see he had an alligator that he was bringing back to the boat. The people got to touch and look at the alligator at very close range. After everyone had a chance to touch and see the alligator, Alicio released the alligator back into the river and then got back in the boat.

Amazed and stunned, the tourists asked, "How did you do that?" Alicio said that he was the most proactive man in the world. The tourists asked him, "What does it take to be the most proactive man in the world?"

Alicio was reported to have said the following six things:

- Be clear about your breakthrough outcome.
- Interrupt your own doubts.
- Recommit to breakthrough results.
- Take personal responsibility.
- Be creative.
- Remember task *and* relationship.

> Courage is not the absence of fear: courage is fear walking
>
> —Susan David, *Emotional Agility* (2016)

For an example of courage, you may not have to look any further than Ernest Shackleton. His voyage to Antarctica in the 1930s was a profile in courage. He ran an ad to hire a crew. How many of you would sign up for this advertisement?

> *Men wanted for hazardous journey.*
> *Low wages, bitter cold, long hours of complete darkness.*
> *Safe return doubtful. Honor and recognition in event of success.*

When the ship was destroyed and survival was doubtful, Shackleton was able to lead all members of the crew to safety. He lost no one. Here are some of the lessons learned from reflecting on this potential disaster:

- Cultivate a sense of compassion and responsibility for others.
- Do your part to help create an upbeat environment at work.
- Broaden your cultural and social horizons beyond your usual experiences.
- In a rapidly changing world, be willing to venture in new directions to seize new opportunities and learn new skills.
- Find a way to turn setbacks and failures to your advantage.
- Be bold in vision and careful in planning.
- Learn from past mistakes—yours and those made by others.
- Never insist on reaching a goal at any cost.
- Don't be drawn into public disputes with rivals.

Courage is about not only having difficult conversations but also confronting behavior of how things have been done and helping people change and modify systems to have more productive results. This is why having the courage to add to your repertoire is so important.

La Salle and Johnson (2019) use the phrase "defining the acceptable floor" in a potent case study in their book *Shattering Inequities*. Leaders are responsible for creating the culture of what is acceptable and what are the lines in the sand. Continuing policies and procedures that are antithetical to equity causes organizations to keep status quo and negative consequences from not addressing foundational issues. It is easier to go along to get along, but that is not necessarily the right thing to do.

Leaders also can model that mistakes are inevitable and to be expected. Courage means mistakes are exposed, confronted, and remediated.

Recovery is more Important than Perfection.

—Michael Grinder

Leaders must confront these four fears:

- fear of being disliked
- fear of conflict
- fear of failure
- fear of being viewed as incompetent

Some strategies to be more effective in dealing with these fears include the following:

- Be clear about your own strong values.
- Name, frame, and tame those fears.
- Confront and acknowledge your fears.
- Create a cadre of trusted colleagues for honest feedback.
- Know that developing courage can be learned.

In closing, we offer the following story to ponder:

A man, his son, and their donkey were walking from one town to another to find someone to buy the donkey—they could not afford to feed it during the approaching winter.

They had not gone far when they passed some travelers heading the other way. As they passed, the miller overheard one of the travelers say, "Look at those fools. With such a healthy donkey, one of them could surely ride."

Not wanting to appear foolish, the miller made his son mount the animal while the miller walked alongside.

After a while, they passed an inn. A group of old men were sitting in the sidewalk cafe sipping coffee, enthusiastically talking. As the miller, his son, and the donkey passed, an old man was overheard saying, "It is just as I have been telling you. The young are lazy and disrespectful of their elders. Look at that healthy boy riding the donkey while his old father walks!"

Again, not wishing to appear disrespected or foolish, the miller asked his son to get off the donkey. The miller climbed onto the donkey. They next met some women coming from town. "Why!" they cried, "your poor little boy is nearly tired out. How can you ride and make him walk?"

Stinging from the criticism, the miller ordered his son to mount the donkey as they both rode.

"Would you believe it!" said another traveler to his companions. "This man is trying to sell his donkey. The poor thing will be exhausted, carrying such a heavy load. What a way to treat an animal!" The miller, again not wanting to appear foolish, got off the donkey. He got some rope and a pole, and, with his son's help, they tied the donkey to the pole and carried him on their shoulders.

Just as they got to town, people came out to witness this ridiculous spectacle. A crowd gathered, laughing, pointing fingers, and shouting. The crowd pressed in closer. On crossing the bridge that led to town, the laughter and shouting so unnerved the donkey that it started to thrash around.

As it struggled, the donkey fell off the bridge and into the water. The unfortunate donkey drowned, and the miller and his son had to walk all the way home, poorer than they had started. In trying to please everyone, they pleased no one, not even themselves.

REFERENCES

Arrien, A. (1993). *The four-fold way: Walking paths of the warrior, teacher, healer, and visionary.* New York: HarperCollins.

David, S. (2016). *Emotional agility: Get unstuck, embrace change, and thrive in work and life.* New York: Avery.

La Salle, R. A., & Johnson, R. S. (2019). *Shattering inequities: Real-world wisdom for school and district leaders.* Lanham, MD: Rowman & Littlefield.

SECTION III

The "WHAT"

What is a goal or vision of success. This is "what" we want to see and hear when successful. It also helps us determine whether we have arrived at the solutions we sought.

What I bring are solutions to problems and challenges for individuals and organizations. These are value-added gifts that a person brings to a situation. The "what" shows that people can count on me to deliver results. All change efforts become personal to the leader who is highly efficacious.

> Do not seek to follow in the footsteps of the wise. Seek what they sought.
> —Matsuo Basho

Chapter 11

Cultural Competence

> The first human necessity is education. For the reason learning is fundamental to social life. Man is born knowing nothing but capable of learning everything. He is subject to what he learns.
>
> —Luis Alberto Machado, *The Right to Be Intelligent* (1980)

We think, as Machado's book title says, everyone has the right to be intelligent. Individuals will benefit from collaboration from many perspectives. How do we elevate better decisions? James Surowiecki (2004) writes, in *The Wisdom of Crowds*, "The more information a group has, the better its collective judgment will be, so you want as many people with good information in a group as possible." Group intelligence can be promoted and used to make better decisions.

Cultural competence is more than hiring more people of color, LGBTQ+, women, and so forth. It is understanding the backgrounds of a diverse workforce, asking questions to learn about their experience, and making sure employees can see a representative population. Equity means ensuring that the diversity has the support to do their best work. This includes leadership that embraces multiple points of view and personal experiences. Inclusion will invite and encourage colleagues to share thoughts and make is easier to contribute to the total quality of the organizational operations.

Why? The more perspectives you consider, the better. Decisions made by a small, cherry-picked group are usually not sustainable. Let's make a point here: There is a difference between role and soul. As a manager or leader, there is a role. That includes evaluating direct reports, making tough budgetary decisions, and challenging negative behavior. Sometimes a manager must put on the role hat and make decisions.

The best managers and leaders have a soul, have empathy, and create psychological safety in the work unit. In education and nonprofits, high relational trust might reduce the likelihood of confrontation. When coaching leaders,

86 Chapter 11

topics of dealing with conflict may feel hard to do. Sometimes they need to put on their role hat.

Surowiecki goes on to say, "Relying on a crowd rather than an individual improves your chances of finding information that you didn't know was out there." Knowing more and getting perspective of more diversity strengthens policies, procedures, and decision-making. The "wisdom of crowds" posits that decisions made by a team are better than decisions made by the smartest person on that team, alone.

Happier people make for a better world. Understanding and embracing diversity extends our relationships and learning. Equity is extremely important. Don't confuse equality with equity. Figure 11.1 provides a visual representation of the difference between equity and equality.

> Treating unequals, equally, is the most unequal thing we do.
>
> —Michael Grinder

As figure 11.1 demonstrates, equal treatment of unequal persons is the most unequal thing we do. Giving everyone the same resources is not equity. Providing what people need to perform their best helps create and sustain equity in the organizational dynamic.

In his book titled *Helping*, Edgar Schein (2009) makes the point to level the playing field to get the best results. People come from different places with

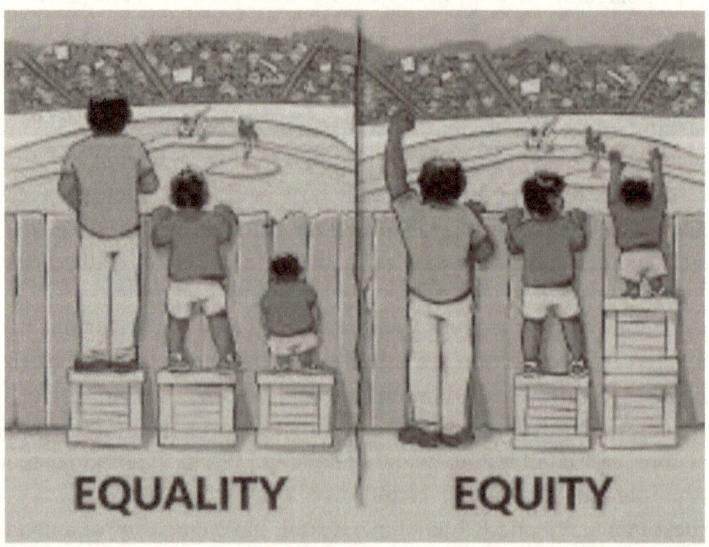

Figure 11.1 Equality versus Equity (*Source*: Art by Angus Maguire; Interaction Institute for Social Change)

different experiences. Find out what they need to be successful. What kind of box or boxes are needed to promote equity?

For our organizations and democracy to thrive, learning is an absolute requirement.

> Every habit can be transformed. He who can be educated can be reeducated. A child becomes what his education is.
>
> —Luis Alberto Machado

Policy manuals may set legal requirements, but what happens when individuals and organizations set reality? Remember what many authors have said: "what we permit, we promote."

Some questions to consider:

- Are you happier and peaceful when you work with people you like?
- Are you happier and peaceful when you have some autonomy about how to do a job?
- Are you happier and peaceful when you have the tools needed to accomplish tasks?

Happy and peaceful is part of *what* people want.

When we listen, we increase our understanding from another's point of view and, most of the time, develop empathy for others. One of the key characteristics that organizations look for in hiring is empathy. The sentiment was expressed eloquently in the 1895 poem, "Judge Softly," by Mary T. Lathrap, a Methodist Episcopal Church preacher and leader in the temperance movement. The poem's best-known line is "just walk a mile in his moccasins."

A message from Akbar's (2020) book *Beyond Ally* comes to mind:

Dear White People,
  No one is asking you to apologize for your ancestors. We are asking you to dismantle the systems of oppression they built, that you maintain and benefit from.

The concept of feedforward, previously mentioned, seems to fit well here. There are major issues of the past that we still grapple with today: Nazis in Germany, slavery in the United States, and the caste system in India. There is not a lot we can do about the past. *But* there is much we can do about the future. Abdicating our responsibility to address policies and procedures that keep negative results in place is not right. There is no right way to do the wrong thing.

> What we think can divide us. What we feel can unite us.
>
> —William Sommers

A colleague once asked, "Is there any end to this learning?" The answer given was "*No.*" When reading the business literature, continuous learning is the secret sauce of the most creative and successful companies.

> The only sustainable competitive advantage is an organization's ability to learn faster than the competition.
>
> —Peter Senge

As a White male, I (Bill) was reading several of the books referred to in this chapter to learn more about microaggressions. I knew about people crossing the street so they did not have to pass a group of Black or Latino kids. However, not understanding this concept at a personal or visceral level, I turned to people I trusted to give me accurate information. First, I turned to my daughter-in-law, who is Afro-Caribbean. I asked her, "Tell me about microaggressions." She told me about people asking to touch her hair while they were already touching her hair. Shocked, I listened to her experiences.

I also repeated this question to a former superintendent with whom I had worked who is an African American. She told me the same thing about her hair. This was a real learning experience for me, as I could not believe that people would violate a person's personal space in such a way. I asked. I listened. I learned.

When you don't know or want to learn something you don't know, *ask*. Then *listen* and *learn*.

> We reward students for getting the right answer, but not for asking good questions.
>
> —Adam Grant

Make positive presuppositions about people. If you are wrong and negative processes are evident, then modify your approaches.

> If you don't believe in them, how do you expect them to see themselves as gifted?
>
> —Fred Bonner II

RESPONSIBLE RISK-TAKING

No one tests the depth of a river with both feet.

—African proverb

Akbar (2020) says, "Taking responsible risks and remaining open to continuous learning requires being an ally first."

Adam Grant, in a recent post, said that at the root of our polarization problem is a deficit of intellectual humility. Too many people refuse to admit that they might be wrong. Diversity of thought opens minds. Intensity of conviction closes them. Knowing your knowledge is incomplete is a prerequisite for learning.

> Equal rights for others does not mean fewer rights for you. This isn't a pie.
>
> —Maysa Akbar, *Beyond Ally* (2020)

Allyship Identity Model: Supporter \ Ally \ Advocate \ Accomplice \ Equity Broker

- **Stage 1: Supporter**. Will you do the right thing, even when no one is watching? Do you recognize that your Whiteness has power? Are you able to be a supporter consistently, without changing your support when White pressure is present?
- **Stage 2: Ally**. Ally identity: allies must lend their voices and their privilege to advance the inclusion and equity for people of color (POCs).
- **Stage 3: Advocate**. Advocate identity: advocates become actively involved in supporting, noting, or leading social justice events with money, time, and resources. Cultural humility sets in during this stage. Cultural humility is a concept developed as a result of the increasing awareness of diversity and the demand for a more inclusive world.
- **Stage 4: Accomplice/Co-conspirator**. Accomplice identity: accomplices work in solidarity with POCs to create and sustain social justice. White accomplices take risks and aren't afraid to put themselves out there to destabilize White supremacy.
- **Stage 5: Equity Broker**. This final stage captures invested equity brokers. Equity broker identity: openly challenges other White people when they are being racist, xenophobic, oppressive, or exercising their privilege. Equity broker characteristics: the ultimate level in the fight for racial justice is building bridges, requiring the privileged to broker opportunities for advancement. I coined the term "equity brokers" to

refer to this top level of alliance and identity. A broker, by definition, negotiates and arranges, acting as an intermediary and mediator.

> People will forget what you said. People will forget what you did. But people will never forget how you made them feel.
>
> —Maya Angelou

> The racial problem is the opportunity gap, as antiracist reformers call it, not the achievement gap.
>
> —Ibram Kendi, *How to Be an Antiracist*

Stefanie Johnson (2020), in her book *Inclusify*, talks about "headwinds" and "tailwinds." Some of us have great support, which is tailwind; it helps move us along. Some have less support in resources and for learning in their lives; these are headwinds that deflate our energy and resources to stay even. How do we level the playing field? How do we accelerate the learning of those with significant headwinds (which are no fault of their own)? How do we amplify those who have "beat the odds"?

Questions for reflection:

- What are the headwinds some colleagues are dealing with?
- What are some of the tailwinds colleagues come to work with?
- How will you provide what each need and want?

Leaders who "inclusify" will have better relationships with their teams, elicit greater productivity from all of their workers, and create a more positive environment for everyone. Johnson has created the ABCs of breaking bias: admit it, block it, count it.

Counting is important because it is follow-up.

Inclusifyers know that their words matter, and they work to learn to communicate more effectively. Being inclusifyed is to stop calling women "girls." Inclusifyers take it upon themselves to update their cultural communication skills. They stay up to date with the business world. Updating one's skills is a common workplace practice.

REFERENCES

Akbar, M. (2020). *Beyond ally.* Hartford, CT: Publish Your Purpose Press.
Johnson, S. (2020). *Inclusify*. New York: HarperCollins.

Kendi, I. X. (2019). *How to be an antiracist.* New York: Penguin.
Machado, L. A. (1980). *The right to be intelligent.* Oxford: Pergamon Press.
Schein, E. (2009). *Helping: How to offer, give, and receive help.* Oakland, CA: Berrett-Koehler.
Surowiecki, J. (2004). *The wisdom of crowds.* New York: Anchor Books.

Chapter 12

Coaching Tools

Our number one coaching tool is Stakeholder Centered Coaching, developed by Marshall Goldsmith and Frank Wagner, both professors of business at UCLA (University of California, Los Angeles). We mentioned this tool in chapter 6.

Question: How many people think life will go back to the way it was in the 1950s, 1960s, and so forth? Rarely do we find anyone who believes we will return to that world. As Bob Dylan sang, "things have changed."

There are things that have not changed, however. Most leaders and organizations want people who are honest, have integrity, make a commitment to work toward common goals, appreciate and embrace diversity, help create solutions to current and future problems, and more.

What has changed is the pace of change, technology advancements, increased interdependency at home and abroad, and unintended consequences resulting from solving problems. As my friend and colleague Michael Ayers (formerly of 3M) says, "Intended consequences sometimes happen; unintended consequences always happen." So, when Goldsmith published his book *What Got You Here Won't Get You There* (2007), he was correct.

STAKEHOLDER CENTERED COACHING

Stakeholder Centered Coaching (SCC) is focused on "feedforward." We can't change the past, *but* we can create a different future depending on what we do. We still rely on what has helped people succeed in the past. The difference is monitoring to make sure the results are consistent with our goals and objectives. If not, then we should change the behaviors to get better results.

Here are some of the tools SCC uses to get positive results:

1. Get feedback from direct reports that the leader trusts.
2. Help the leader accept the good and challenging comments.

3. Establish a system that shortens the feedback loop.
4. Apologize, if necessary, for past transgressions.
5. Make public efforts to get better.
6. Follow up with colleagues and direct reports.
7. Actively listen and say "thank you" for providing feedback.
8. Continue to focus on behaving in alignment with what the leader has committed to do.

Marshall Goldsmith, Frank Wagner, and Chris Coffey (who has since passed away) said the leader can say they have changed. The real issue is, does the referent group believe the leader has changed? *And* does the change continue over time?

A major requirement is follow-up. Without follow-up, not much will change. When coaching others, it is important to begin with the commitments that were made during the last call or meeting. Numerous sources identify follow-up as critical in continuous improvement.

- Follow-up is how you measure your progress.
- Follow-up is how our efforts cement behavior changes in our colleagues' minds.
- Follow-up is how to increase the belief that change is permanent.
- Follow-up holds us accountable and responsible.

BUSINESS REVIEW PLAN

> Coming together is a beginning; keeping together is progress; working together is success.
>
> —Henry Ford

The Business Review Plan (BRP) was used by Alan Mulally as he turned around two iconic corporations: first Boeing, and then Ford. As Mulally considered the move from Boeing to Ford, he asked why Ford wanted to hire him. The answer was to get someone with vision. Mulally wrote two things on his notepad:

Compelling vision
Ruthless execution

Both vision and execution are needed for a responsive organization. As I (Bill) like to say, "Knowledge is important and insufficient."

Mullaly implemented the BRP for the leaders to check progress. Initially leaders were reluctant to identify lack of progress. Eventually, one leader took a risk of telling the group that the unit was struggling to perform. Mulally applauded this honesty.

A list of ten rules was posted on the wall:

1. People first
2. Everyone is included
3. Compelling vision
4. Clear performance goals
5. One plan
6. Facts and data
7. Propose a plan, "find-a-way" attitude
8. Respect, listen, help, and appreciate each other
9. Emotional resilience . . . trust the process
10. Have fun . . . enjoy the journey and each other

> The teacher will appear when the student is ready.
>
> —Buddhist maxim

The process Mulally established was as follows:

1. Determine the metrics to assess progress.
2. Report the results each week by color-coding them (green for positive, yellow for caution, and red for moving backward).
3. The team provides possible actions to turn yellow or red to green. It is everyone's responsibility as team leaders.
4. Report back on what is working and what strategies have not produced the results desired.

The BRP focused on what they could do moving forward. It accelerated the growth of Ford, created more trust among the leaders, and cascaded into the culture of the company.

TRILLION DOLLAR COACH

This process is about a coach named Bill Campbell. He was a football coach for a high school years ago. He ended up coaching CEOs such as Eric Schmidt of Google and Steve Jobs of Apple. He was a no-nonsense person with strong values. The following are some of the tools he used as a coach.

Google developed Project Aristotle, which unleashed creativity and innovation.

The five key factors Project Aristotle focused on could have been taken right out of Bill Campbell's playbook.

1. Excellent teams at Google had psychological safety (people knew that if they took risks, their manager would have their back).
2. The teams had clear goals, each role was meaningful, and members were reliable and confident that the team's mission would make a difference.
3. Build safety.
4. Clarity and meaning.
5. Dependability and impact into each team he coached.

Leaders must enforce adherence to the norms established for the team to operate at an optimum level. "A 2014 study finds that it is the most insecure managers who are threatened by suggestions from others (in other words, coaching)."

> Your title makes you a manager. Your people will decide if you're a leader, and it's up to you to live up to that.
>
> —Bill Campbell (from Schmidt, Rosenberg, & Eagle [2019])

Noel Tichy and Eli Cohen (1997) wrote *The Leadership Engine*. Tichy was at the General Electric innovation site in Crotonville, New York. He said that leaders have two main responsibilities:

- Be the head learner.
- Develop other leaders.

We have found, by employing coaching tools, that leadership development can elevate leadership, build trust faster, and produce better results for the organization. Coaching can also be a leading indicator of whether a person is ready to progress. As Peter Drucker, the famous leadership guru, said, "The leader of the past tells people what to do, and the leader of the future asks questions."

People want to be listened to, taken seriously, and know that you have a genuine interest in what they are saying. Running effective meetings will increase meaning and take less time.

One of the toughest problems managers must deal with is what to do with the person who's a star performer and difficult to work with. "You get these quirky guys or women who are going to be great differentiators for you. It is your job to manage that person in a way that doesn't disrupt the company" (Schmidt, Rosenberg, & Eagle, 2019). Dealing with these people effectively is hard but worthwhile, as long as the behavior is not destructive to the goals and team. The goal is more genius but less aberrant. Highly creative and intelligent people can provide quick insights into what barriers exist and contribute creative solutions. If there is "too much ego," that will be a problem the leader must confront.

Teams can have disagreements. Emotional conflict must be kept in check to produce the best results. "Teams that trust each other will still have disagreements, but when they do, they will be accompanied by less emotional rancor." Google studied factors that contribute to high-functioning teams. Psychological safety came out of top. See Amy Edmondson's *Fearless Organization* (2019) for a deeper dive into the research.

Research by Daniel McAllister of Georgetown University demonstrates that trust increases with more contact between the manager and a peer. Here are Bill Campbell's suggestions for next steps in coaching people:

- *Be creative*. After age fifty should be your most creative time. You have wisdom of experience and freedom to apply it where you want.
- *Don't be a dilettante*. Don't do résumé building. Get involved with meaningful projects and make a positive impact.
- *Apply your gifts*. What are the strengths that make you stand out? Apply those strengths to a purpose that drives you.
- *Quit worrying about the future*. As Mary Catherine Bateson said, "life is improvisation." Make the most of it.

SITUATIONAL LEADERSHIP

Prescription without diagnosis is malpractice.

—James Muir

Paul Hersey developed the "Situational Leadership" model. Some people are ready and willing; some people are highly skilled. Apply the right strategy for the situation. An adaptation can be seen in figure 12.1.

Knowing which quadrant the individual or team is in helps predict what coaching/support process may be best for the situation. Leadership is influence. The leader who has the most flexibility can access and motivate a wider group of people. You can't rely on one way to do leading, coaching, supporting, or delegating. The more repertoire, the more influence.

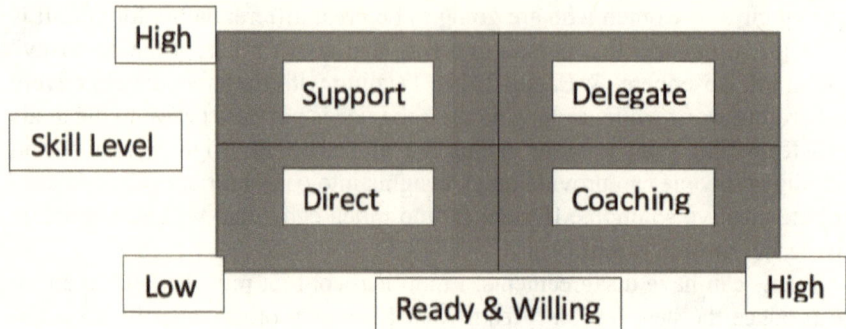

Figure 12.1 Ready, Willing, and Able (*Source*: Sommers [2021]; image created with aid from Michael Ayers)

REFERENCES

Edmondson, A. (2019). *The fearless organization*. Hoboken, NJ: John Wiley & Sons.

Goldsmith, M. (2007). *What got you here won't get you there: How successful people become even more successful*. New York: Hyperion.

Hersey, P. (2004). *The situational leader* (4th ed.). Escondido, CA: Center for Leadership Studies, Inc.

McAllister, Daniel J. (1995). Affect- and cognition-based trust as foundations for interpersonal cooperation in organizations. *Academy of Management Journal*, 38(1), 24–59.

Schmidt, E., Rosenberg, J., & Eagle, A. (2019). *Trillion dollar coach: The leadership handbook of Silicon Valley's Bill Campbell*. New York: HarperCollins.

Sommers, W. (2021). *Creating talent density*. Lanham, MD: Rowman & Littlefield.

Tichy, N. M., & Cohen, E. B. (1997). *The leadership engine: How winning companies build leaders at every level*. New York: Harper Business.

Chapter 13

Commonwealth

Michael Ayers (2002) defines a commonwealth as "organizations achieving their goals for the common good." He began with the following: "There is no power equal to a community discovering what it cares about." So, the question we start with is "What do you and your community care about?" Ayers's manuscript is titled *Ordinary Leadership* because it is a handbook for what leadership could and should normally be in communities and organizations. Leadership is *not* different in social services, education, nonprofits, and business. Leadership is influence and actions.

Tichy and Cohen (1997) write, "Learning, teaching and leading are inextricably intertwined." We resist the idea that there are different sets of values, policies, and procedures for employees and leaders. There are different roles. As a leader, supervising, evaluating, budgeting, and so on are part of the role and require decision-making. The best examples in business and education have shared leadership. Leaders especially have a position to model the beliefs and actions that help bring the heart, hands, and feet to the organization. This process requires a merging of "role and soul."

Leaders have defined roles with responsibilities attached. At the same time, colleagues want to know whether the leader has a soul. This is where honesty and vulnerability can bridge the gap between having the role and having humanity.

Two thousand years ago, the philosopher Seneca wrote (as quoted by Ryan Holiday in *The Daily Stoic*):

> What gives me pleasure in learning something is that I can teach it. Nothing will ever please me, not even what is remarkably beneficial, if I have learned it for myself only. If wisdom were given to me with this proviso, that I should keep it shut up in myself and never express it to anyone else, I should refuse it, no good is enjoyable to possess without a companion.

When a leader is a learner, a collaborator, and is willing to share decision-making, more trust and allegiance is formed. Leadership is not all about the leader; it is equally or more about the colleagues.

Learning and leading exist in community. We repeat, "knowledge is important *and* insufficient." If learning doesn't lead to an advancement of the mission of the organization, how does learning help? Learning Omnivores (www.learningomnivores.com) is committed to extending and expanding learning that will contribute to a better world. Remember from biology that carnivores eat meat, herbivores eat plants, and omnivores eat it all. Learning Omnivores can and will learn from anyone, anything, any time and share it.

Let's start with a graphic (figure 13.1) that can be a foundation for organizations and leaders, which can be summed up as follows:

- Vision—the optimal goal. It is the combination of people, actions, and values.
- Mission—how the individuals, groups, or organization deliver. It is an intersection of actions and values.
- Values—how we will act while working to accomplish the mission.
- Trust—the belief that people will act in accordance with stated values.
- Action—how people behave and what their skill level is.
- Expertise—people have knowledge and skills demonstrate by the actions they take.

In his book *Community*, Peter Block (2009) provides several key points. He posits that belonging can be interpreted as a longing to be. People want to know where they fit in the organization and where they can contribute. Herzberg (1987) listed, over forty years ago, the intrinsic motivators:

- achievement

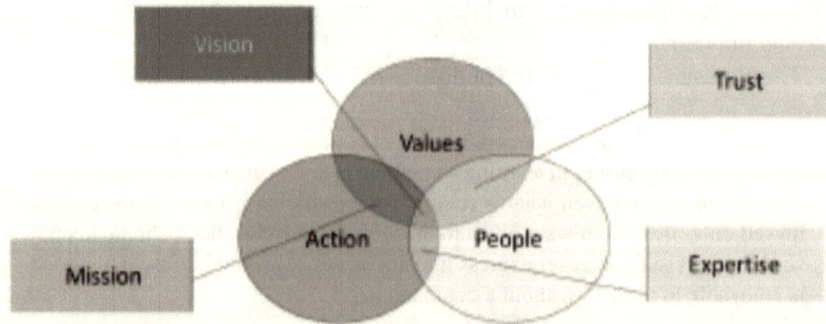

Figure 13.1 Intersection Model (*Source*: Printed by permission from Michael Ayers, *Ordinary Leadership* [2002])

- recognition for achievement, the work itself
- responsibility
- growth or advancement

Being recognized for the contributions to a common goal builds group consensus and interdependence. Both are important in creating a positive work environment. Peter Block (2009) said, "Community is the container within which our longing to be is fulfilled." Building community shifts the focus from individual to the greater whole. Again, Block's quote seems to fit here: "The essential challenge is to transform the isolation and self-interest within our community into connectedness and caring for the whole. The key is to identify how this transformation occurs. We begin by shifting our attention from the problems and community to the possibility of community." This process grows the social capital for a community of learners, leaders, and legacy.

One of the great questions that can be asked at the beginning of meetings for working groups comes from Kathie Dannemiller: "How will the world be different tomorrow as a result of our meeting today?" The answers provide insight into the work and the outcomes desired. We cannot mandate the heart of the community. We must create the bond and the reciprocity that makes work enjoyable with the commitment to the group.

So, "What can we create together?" This question requires a shift in focus from me to us. Here are a few more shifts of focus from the work of Peter Block (2009):

- from problems to possibilities
- from fear and fault to gifts, generosity, and abundance
- from law and oversight to social fabric and chosen accountability
- from corporation and systems to associational life
- from leaders to citizens

Every one of us has gifts and talents that can add value.

> Stop labeling others for their deficiencies and focus on their gifts.
>
> —Peter Block

Leaders increase influence in three ways:

1. They shift the context when people gather.
2. They name the conversation to have thorough, powerful questions.
3. They listen rather than advocate or defend.

Here are some questions Block suggests for creating the culture or the container of meetings and working:

- What is the commitment you hold that brought you into this room?
- What is the price you or others are paying for being here today?
- How valuable do you plan for this effort to be?
- What is the crossroads you face at this stage of the game?
- What is the story you keep telling about the problems of this community?
- What are the gifts you hold that have not been brought fully into the world?
- What is your contribution to the very thing you complain about?
- What is it about you or your team, group, or neighborhood that no one knows?

Most of us have heard that people best create when they own the problem and the solutions.

William Bridges (1991) is famous for his work on transitions. If we shift the context and build a new container, how does that occur? Bridges would suggest that there is an ending first, followed by a neutral phase, and then a new beginning.

Vignette

A new principal was hired to change a school culture after two years of turmoil. The new principal heard from staff and organizational leaders about issues that kept emerging and getting worse. The new principal asked some staff members how the year ended. The answer was along the lines of "the former principal presided over graduation, walked off the stage, and nobody saw them after that."

> New principal: What changes had occurred since then?
>
> Leadership team: The large school had twenty staff members who either retired or were let go.
>
> New principal: What happened to them?
>
> Leadership team: We don't know.
>
> New principal: It doesn't sound like the school had honorable closure. Before being introduced to the faculty, we must close last year.
>
> Leadership team: We must find a current staff member who knows the departed staff member and have the current staff member prepare a short message about where the departed staff member is and how they are doing.

New principal: Then the superintendent will introduce me formally to the staff. We will be in the neutral zone, which is very uncomfortable.

Leadership team: The staff will not know at the outset what new ideas will surface.

New principal: We will build this culture together with new protocols.

Building sustainable, positive cultures is very hard work *and* very important work. When change occurs, there is a feeling of the "devil known is better than the devil unknown." Leaders create cultures through their words and, more important, their deeds. Hire the hands, engage the heart, and watch the feet.

REFERENCES

Ayers, M. (2002). *Ordinary leadership*. Unpublished manuscript.

Block, P. (2009). *Community: The structure of belonging*. Oakland, CA: Berrett-Koehler.

Bridges, W. (1991). *Managing transitions—making the most of change*. New York: Addison-Wesley.

Herzberg, F. (1987/2003). One more time: How do you motivate employees? One more time: Best of HBR (article reprints on hbr.org). *Harvard Business Review* (January), pp. 2–12.

Tichy, N. M., & Cohen, E. B. (1997). *The leadership engine: How winning companies build leaders at every level*. New York: Harper Business.

Conclusion
Next Steps

Run the experiment.

—Richard Sheridan, Menlo Innovations

First, try something. As W. Edwards Deming said long ago, you are getting 100 percent of the results you are designed to get. One of the quotes Sheridan often uses is "run the experiment"—meaning, try something. When I (Bill) was asked, "What have you learned in thirty-five years of leadership?" I answered, "If it isn't working, try something else."

At the end of this book, you are reminded to stay consistent on your path. First, ask questions, courageously initiate discussions, be sincerely curious about people, and show respect and humility. People will appreciate your attitude and want to be around you because you add positive value to their daily lives.

Second, keep reading and learning. Many solutions come from implementing ideas from one area and adapting it to another. Velcro came from removing burrs from a dog's hair. Airbag technology came from hand grenades. Lots of ideas come from outside our field of work.

Third, tell someone about what you are finding out. To quote Joseph Joubert, "To teach is to learn twice." Write down thoughts on a white board. People will ask what that idea is about. Then you get to explain and deepen your understanding.

Don't leave your life to chance or fate. Remember that through your actions, you initiate a course of events that, as a consequence, like the movement of a butterfly's wings in another part of the world, can do great things in your life and career.

The two of us—Jakub Grządzielski, from the engineering/business world, and Bill Sommers, from the education world—came together to write this book. Find a partner or a group, and start working on a problem. The creativity of diversity and trust can produce amazing results.

Try it; you'll like it.

FINAL THOUGHTS

We hope you have enjoyed this journey. Now it is your turn to make some of these ideas a reality in your context. As Peter Block's book title says, *The Answer to How Is Yes*. So, what do you say yes to? By saying, "Yes, I'll try this," you eliminate some other options. Say *"yes"* and get moving.

You can permanently improve your quality of life by choosing daily learning and self-improvement as a way for your beautiful career and life journey. We wish you well on your journey to create a culture of coaching, creativity, and collaboration.

Index

accuracy—probing for specificity, 54–55
Achor, Shawn, 13
Adapt or Die (Lynch), 1
affective conflict, 57
Akbar, Maysa, 87, 89
Alder, Shannon L., 6
allyship identity model, 89–90
Amason, Allen C., 57
Andelson, Steven, 45
Angelou, Maya, 90
Annunzio, Susan Lucia, 77
The Answer to How Is Yes (Block), 106
Arrien, Angeles, 21, 78, 79
Axelrod, Dick, 33–34
Axelrod, Emily, 33–34
Ayers, Michael, 34, 93, 98, 99

Bailey, Suzanne, 24
Bandura, Albert, 38
Basho, Matsuo, 83
Bateson, Mary Catherine, 97
Beckhard, Richard, 3, 24, 66
Be Open Minded (PBS program), 30
Beyer, Damon, 26
Beyond Ally (Akbar), 87, 89
Block, Peter, 33, 38, 100, 101–102, 106
Blum-DeStefano, Jessica, 19, 23, 38
Bonner, Fred, II, 88

Boughton, Harold, 14
BrainTrust (Pixar), 35
Bridges, William, 3, 66, 102
Business Review Plan (BRP), 35, 94–95

Campbell, Bill. *See* trillion dollar coach
Carnegie, Dale, 12
Catmull, Ed, 72–73
CHaD (courage, humility, and discipline), 34
Chadwick, Bob, 26
change, 5, 6, 24, 65–68; managing, 67; models, 66. *See also* Bailey, Suzanne; Beckhard, Richard; Kotter, John; Lippitt, Mary
Clark, Karen, 1
coaching, 22–23; instructional, 42–44; strategies, 34–36; and supervision, 37–46; tools, 20, 93–98
Coffey, Chris, 2, 3, 94
cognitive conflict, 57
Cohen, Eli, 12, 96, 99
collaboration, 21–22; facilitating, 33–36
collective efficacy. *See* efficacy
commonwealth, 99–103
communication, 20–21, 29–30
Community (Block), 100, 101
community, 99, 100–101

conflict, 23–24, 49–63; affective versus cognitive, 57; management strategies, 23; polarity partnerships, 51–53
courage, 26–27, 77–82. *See also* leadership, courageous
Creating Talent Density (Sommers), 34
creativity, 25–26, 69–75
Creativity, Inc. (Catmull), 72–73
cultural competence, 85–90
cultural humility, 89
cultural responsiveness, 20

Dalio, Ray, 50, 62
Dannemiller, Kathleen D., 3, 101
data, 44
David, Susan, 9, 80
defining the acceptable floor, 80
Deming, W. Edwards, 2, 15, 105
Dewey, John, 74
Dintersmith, Ted, 11
Distributed Leadership (Spillane), 12
Diversity of Life (Wilson), 25
Drago-Severson, Eleanor, 19, 23, 37–38
Drucker, Peter, 40, 75, 96

Edmondson, Amy, 57, 97
efficacy, 38
Einstein, Albert, 25, 70
Emotional Agility (David), 9, 80
emotional blackmail, 57, 59–61
equality versus equity, 86
extended learning options for Learning Omnivores, 35

Fearless Organization (Edmondson), 97
fears, 81
feedforward, 44, 45, 87, 93
Felps, Will, 46, 49
Flawless Consulting (Block), 33
Ford, Henry, 94
Forward, Susan, 59–60
foundational skills, 54
The Four-Fold Way (Arrien), 78

The Four Obsessions of an Extraordinary Executive (Lencioni), 13
FRISK (facts, rule, impact, suggestions, knowledge), 45–46
Fullan, Michael, 65
Future Shock (Toffler), 6

gameboard of change model, 24
Gandhi, Mohandas, 5
Gardner, John, 13–14
Garfield, Charles, 38
Garmston, Bob, 25
Get There Early (Johansen), 2
goal setting, 6–7, 44
Goethe, Wolfgang, 79
Goldsmith, Marshall, 1, 2, 5, 34, 37, 44–45, 58, 78, 93, 94
Google: Project Aristotle, 96; Work Rules, 35
Gottman's Successful Marriage, 57–58
Grant, Adam, 88, 89
Greater Purpose Statement, 52
Grinder, Michael, 81, 86
Grządzielski, Jakub, 12, 51, 70, 105

Hard Things about Hard Things (Horowitz), 46
Hard Won Wisdom (Janove), 46
Hattie, John, 38
headwinds, 90
Heath, Chip, 75
Heath, Dan, 75
Helping (Schein), 38, 39–40, 86–87
Hemingway, Ernest, 14
Hersey, Paul, 34, 97
Herzberg, F., 100–101
Hightower, Jim, 27
Hord, Shirley M., 1
Horowitz, Ben, 46
How to Win Friends and Influence People (Carnegie), 12
Humble Consulting (Schein), 42
Humble Inquiry (Schein), 38, 39, 40–42

Impact Cycle, 42–44
Inclusify (Johnson), 90
instructional coaching. *See* coaching, instructional
Intersection Model, 100

Jacobs, Robert W., 3
Janove, Jathan, 46
Jobs, Steve, 5, 95
Johansen, Bob, 2
Johnson, Ruth, 80
Johnson, Stefanie, 90
Joni, Saj-nicole, 26
Joubert, Joseph, 105
"Judge Softly" (Lathrap), 87

Kendi, Ibram, 90
Kettering, Charles F., 55
Kierkegaard, Søren, 37
Killer Bs (budgets, boundaries, and bosses), 16
Klein, Gary, 73
Knight, Jim, 42, 43
The Knowing-Doing Gap (Pfeffer and Sutton), 14–15
Kotter, John, 66, 74

Lam, David, 3
La Salle, Robin Avelar, 80
Lathrap, Mary T., 87
leaders, responsibilities, 4, 12–14, 96
leadership: basics of, 11–16; courageous, 26; situational, 34, 35, 97–98
The Leadership Engine (Tichy and Cohen), 12, 96, 99
learning cultures, seven Cs of, 19–27
Learning Omnivores, 35, 100
Lencioni, Patrick, 13, 14, 30
Let's Stop Meeting Like This (Axelrod and Axelrod), 33–34
Lippitt, Mary, 24, 66, 67
Lippman, Walter, 75
Lively Ls (learning, leading, and lasting relationships), 16

Livesay, John, 30, 63
locus of control. *See* efficacy
Lynch, Rick, 1

Machado, Luis Alberto, 85, 87
Managing Transitions (Bridges), 3
managing up, 58–59
McAllister, Daniel, 97
McLuhan, Marshall, 20, 29
The Medium Is the Message (McLuhan), 29
meeting canoe, 33–34
meetings, 41; effective, 21, 33–34, 96
Meta-Model/Specificity Model, 55
mistakes, 56
Mitroff, Ian, 74
Muir, James, 34, 97
Mulally, Alan, 35, 94–95

Native Wisdom for White Minds (Schaef), 30
Netflix, 35
The New IQ (Coffey and Lam), 3
Nightingale, Earl, 6
Nine Professional Conversations to Change Our Schools (Sommers and Zimmerman), 22–23, 26

Olsen, Walter R., 22, 30
On Leadership (Gardner), 13–14
Ordinary Leadership (Ayers), 99
Our Iceberg Is Melting (Kotter), 66, 74

Peak Performers (Garfield), 38
Peterson, Dennis, 26
Pfeffer, Jeffrey, 14–15
Picasso, Pablo, 78
Pixar, 35, 72
The Power of Moments (Heath and Heath), 75
Principles (Dalio), 50
Project Aristotle. *See* Google

reflection, 39–42
The Right Fight (Joni and Beyer), 26

The Right to Be Intelligent (Machado), 85
Roosevelt, Theodore, 7
Rotter, Julian, 38

SCC. *See* Stakeholder Centered Coaching
Schaef, Anne Wilson, 30
Schein, Edgar, 38, 39–42, 86–87
self-efficacy. *See* efficacy
Seneca, Lucius Annaeus, 99
Senge, Peter, 13, 88
Sense of Urgency (Kotter), 66
Shackleton, Ernest, 80
Shattering Inequities (La Salle and Johnson), 80
Shedd, John, 74
Sheridan, Richard, 11, 12, 13, 14–15, 21, 105
Shinseki, Eric, 65
Sinek, Simon, 9, 15, 17
situational leadership. *See* leadership, situational
Slap, Stan, 21–22
Smart Thinking for Crazy Times (Mitroff), 74
Sommers, William A., 1, 4, 9, 11, 19, 88, 105; *Creating Talent Density*, 34, 98; *Nine Professional Conversations to Change Our Schools*, 22–23, 26; *A Trainer's Companion*, 22, 30
Spillane, James, 12
Stakeholder Centered Coaching (SCC), 2, 37, 40, 44–45, 93–94

STAR (save time—add repertoire), 38
Start with Why (Sinek), 9
Stroop, John Ridley, 74
Suicide Spear, 77–78
Surowiecki, James, 85, 86
Sutton, Robert I., 14–15

tailwinds, 90
Tell Me So I Can Hear You (Drago-Severson and Blum-DeStefano), 19, 23, 37–38
Tichy, Noel, 12, 96, 99
Toffler, Alvin, 6, 67
Tolstoy, Leo, 7
A Trainer's Companion (Olsen and Sommers), 22, 30
trillion dollar coach (Bill Campbell): process, 35, 95–97

VUCA (volatility, uncertainty, complexity, ambiguity), 2

Wagner, Frank, xi, 2, 93, 94
What Got You Here Won't Get You There (Goldsmith), 1, 44, 93
What Schools Should Be (Dintersmith), 11
Wilson, Edward O., 25
The Wisdom of Crowds (Surowiecki), 85
word ball, 71–72

Zimmerman, Diane P., 22–23, 26, 46

About the Authors

William A. Sommers, PhD, of Austin, Texas, continues to be a learner, teacher, principal, author, leadership coach, and consultant. Bill has come out of retirement multiple times to put theory into practice as a principal in high schools and middle schools. He has worked at inner city schools as well as in high-socioeconomic-status suburban districts. Bill has been a consultant for cognitive coaching, adaptive schools, brain research, poverty, habits of mind, conflict management, and classroom management strategies and is a Marshall Goldsmith–certified Stakeholder Centered Coach.

Bill served on the board of trustees of the National Staff Development Council (now Learning Forward) for five years and as president for one year. He is the former executive director for secondary curriculum and professional learning for Minneapolis Public Schools and a school administrator for more than thirty-five years. He has also been a senior fellow for the Urban Leadership Academy at the University of Minnesota. Bill has served as an adjunct faculty member at Texas State University, Hamline University, University of St. Thomas, St. Mary's University, Union Institute, and Capella University. In addition, he has been a program director for an adolescent chemical dependency treatment center and on the board of a halfway house for twenty years.

Bill has coauthored ten books: *Living on a Tightrope: A Survival Handbook for Principals*; *Becoming a Successful Principal: How to Ride the Wave of Change without Drowning*; *Reflective Practice to Improve Schools*; *A Trainer's Companion*; *Energizing Staff Development Using Video Clips*; *Leading Professional Learning Communities*; *Guiding Professional Learning Communities*; *Principal's Field Manual*; *A Trainer's Companion for Habits of Mind*; and *Nine Professional Conversations to Change Schools*. Bill has also coauthored chapters in several other books.

To learn more about Bill's work, visit www.learningomnivores.com or follow him @BillSommers8 on Twitter.

Jakub Grządzielski is an insightful and effective executive and leadership coach with a unique corporate executive background, who meets other executives with a resonate voice of experience. He is a Marshall Goldsmith–certified Stakeholder Centered Coach.

Specializing in one-on-one coaching engagements with senior executives, entrepreneurs, leadership teams, and high potentials, he serves as an ally to personal and professional development, speaking power to truth to provoke possibilities for empowered growth. With Grządzielski's assistance, clients surpass set goals, thrive, and create sustainable success for themselves, their teams, and their organizations.

Grządzielski's mission is to coach executives—true leaders who want to help build a world in which the vast majority of people wake up every day inspired to step into their greatness; feel safe, supported, and cared about when they are at their jobs; and return safely home to their families and friends feeling fulfilled by the lives they've touched and the work they do.

He may be reached by email: jakub.grzadzielski@gmail.com.

www.ingramcontent.com/pod-product-compliance
Lightning Source LLC
Chambersburg PA
CBHW021800230426
43669CB00006B/144